THE EVENT
PROFESSIONAL'S
HANDBOOK

THE EVENT
PROFESSIONAL'S
HANDBOOK

2017004238

HARRIMAN HOUSE LTD
18 College Street
Petersfield
Hampshire
GU31 4AD
GREAT BRITAIN
Tel: +44 (0)1730 233870

Email: contact@harriman-house.com
Website: www.harriman-house.com

First published in Great Britain in 2016.
Each chapter remains copyright © of the respective author.

The right of the authors to be identified as the Authors has been asserted in accordance with the Copyright, Designs and Patents Act 1988.

ISBN: 978-0-85719-510-4

British Library Cataloguing in Publication Data
A CIP catalogue record for this book can be obtained from the British Library.

CONTENTS

FOREWORD

Our lives are punctuated throughout by events and experiences. They help us to make sense of the past by creating memories and to picture a future of endless opportunities through inspiration and engagement. There has never been a better time to be immersed in this multifaceted industry, with Bellwether reports consistently showing growth and renewed focus on the power of events to deliver for brands, organisations and individuals. Those professionals who strive to both conceive and deliver events are a fairly unique group. Showing unrivalled levels of commitment and energy, they are natural problem solvers with a flare for communication and a passion for putting on the best show.

The role of *The Event Professional's Handbook* is not simply to inspire, but to guide and encourage. Its contributors represent some of the most interesting thinkers and practitioners in the industry today. But the handbook is not a 'how to' or an instruction manual. It's more like a smorgasbord of event professionals' thoughts and ideas, designed to whet the appetite, provide a moment of insight or a way of navigating a challenge in a new way.

There is no doubt a tangible value in the diversity of contribution and perspectives. Stories that will not only help you the reader to think more deeply about the future of our industry, but you will also find personal accounts of career-defining decisions that led to further opportunities both professionally and beyond...I met my wife working on a large-scale event pitch for example.

Read this book with an open and curious mind and you are sure to be rewarded. If it motivates one student to start their journey or helps another established event professional through a sticky patch it will have done its job.

Enjoy!

Jason Megson
Vice President, Managing Director
George P. Johnson

EVENTS: CREATING
EMOTIONAL
MEMORABILIA,
FROM BAND
TO
BRAND

KEVIN JACKSON
DIRECTOR OF IDEAS AND
INNOVATION, THE EXPERIENCE IS
THE MARKETING

The motivation for this book is simple; my aim is for everyone to realise the opportunity that is before us. Needless to say, I really do believe that the Experience *is* the Marketing, and furthermore, I believe that everything we are currently doing as #EventProfs will be the future of *all* marketing.

The world has changed, and the thing that we humans value most right now are those moments in which we are actively creating shared experiences. Experience is what leaves us most fulfilled, what we enjoy most, and what big brands are beginning to notice the value in investing in. What's happened in the last ten years of this industry is that we've moved from just events to creating real experiences, and as digital and social have become more important in the ecosystem of these experiences, there's an increasing need to delve deeper and harness these opportunities for growth within each individual company, and indeed, each individual, to take clients to bigger and better places.

This book is about trying to ensure that we can all understand and recognise our part in this journey, however small it may be. For us all, what we do has to be important, it has to move a brand forward, and it always has to connect with people in unique and dynamic ways. After all, we're a people industry. And the one thing that will always unite people is the need to gather, and the need to tell stories. And as long as we can also prove our value and develop new ways to measure the impact of what we do, the only way for this industry is up. What we need to do next is to show how our work matters, and the only way client companies and brands prove their value is return on investment (ROI). And of course ROI doesn't have to always be money, but it has to always be measured. You have to know where you started and where you finished and the gap in between is what value you added. As long as we in the experience marketing industry understand that we can provide value and prove value to our clients, then we will be starting to move up the evolutionary chain of agencies that are involved with clients.

When I first started in industry, in advertising, we were the main thrust of all marketing. But now clients understand that not only is marketing a collective, a collaboration of agencies involved in providing solutions and driving their brands forward, but also the emphasis has changed from a passive medium like advertising, to an active medium like an event. You can shake hands with your customers, consumers and clients, you can get instant feedback and reaction, you can create an emotional connection between you, the brand and the audiences that sustain you. As long as you've got that emotional connection with your audiences, you will sustain and continue to grow and prosper as a brand.

As I've spoken at universities in the last year and a half, what I've tried to do for students running through event management degrees is to give them a sense of what's going to happen to them the day they leave. As I float round academia, I usually ask the students 'Hands up everyone who was motivated to come into the events industry by going to Glastonbury?' and 90% of them put their hands up. And that's where that emotional connection comes from and I try and point out that while 90% were inspired by the music industry, 95% of them will end up working in a corporate market.

And that means a different mindset – understanding what the brand is trying to do, what the context of the event is, what does the brand stand for and then what does the audience want to feel, think and do. Once you've got all those things you can create a successful event. Which isn't the same motivation as a rock festival, but believe it or not, they end up being in similar places. Fresh talent might be first drawn to events because of the dazzling show, as that's where you can most clearly see the emotion transmitted through the power of a live event. But then when they begin their education, that's when it becomes clear that these skills are transferable across so many other realms they wouldn't necessarily even think about.

That's how I first got involved. I saw the power of that connection and wanted to bring that into the brand arena. It doesn't matter why you come into events or brand experiences, it matters what you do when you get there. And you've got to create that emotional link. That's the power behind it all. And that's why brands invest in it, because it's unique. Everyone's been to a gig before where they've come out and said 'that was amazing, I've had the best time of my life' but people do go to conferences and launch events and say exactly the same thing.

And I suppose for us, what happens at the end of the gig is you go and buy the merchandise, that's what connects you to the emotional experience you just had. And so what we need to do in the event industry is the same. To follow up and sustain and to create some 'merchandise' that they can own and touch to keep them connected. We as brand management need to keep that community alive and foster that emotional connection to the benefit of all, not just the benefit of the brand. The future of the events industry is about creating emotional memorabilia that solidifies the live event as one of the most powerful marketing tools a brand could have in its arsenal.

THERE'S ALWAYS GOING TO BE THE

HUMAN NEED

TO GATHER

AND

WE CAN TRY TO

CREATE

ANOTHER UNDERSTANDING OF IT

DEBS ARMSTRONG
CEO, STRONG & CO

The thing I always remember about events, is that every person is just a spoke in the bigger wheel – even if you're the spoke who co-ordinates the others.

The events industry is incredibly broad: it includes everything from private parties for individuals, to conferences; and from B2B and internal events for corporations to festivals, concerts and immersive theatrical events. But what unites most of the people working in them, is that they have a passion for people and they have a passion for making stuff happen under extreme circumstances. At the core of any good Event Director is being able to pull together all these passionate people around a central vision in harmony, because after all, clever people doing what they love equals a great event.

In this industry, you build a strong familial connection with people because you go through such extreme situations together. This is not a job where you clock in at 9am then clock off at 5pm and go to the pub. You're likely to end up in really tricky live event situations, or Health and Safety nightmares, or things that require you to be up all night, sweating and crying with your team. I remember vividly the first year we ran Lost Vagueness at Glastonbury. It was 2am. I was still in the production office and it was chucking it down with rain and miserable, and I look out the door and there's one guy digging a ditch in the rain and then someone else comes in and sticks a Post-it note on the top of my head that says "remember we love you". You can't help but bond through those things. You know who is there for you and you never forget those who helped you.

Everything I've learnt in my career, I've learnt from clever people who just know what they're talking about. And if there's something I don't know, I'll always find a clever person and get them to mentor me. I've had many mentors and to this day I could never narrow it down to just one person who's helped to educate me.

I'll learn a lot from a smart lawyer, a lot from a smart businessman, a lot from a smart broker – it all depends on what I need to develop. Sometimes I think "In order to make this project successful, what do I need to know?" If I don't know anything about, say, global licensing, I'll think "Who's a global licensing expert? Can I reach out in my networks?" Who do I know, or who do I know that knows someone that might get the vision, and be up for sharing their knowledge with me?

Mentors are crucial in this industry as they give you a lot more confidence, and, for example, in a key negotiation they might have given you something which gives you that edge. They help you curate a specialised set of skills from people who are experts in their fields.

With that, I can't understate the importance of a network. I find almost all my new talent through existing respected contacts. People do approach me directly, but largely it's through my network. We generally end up life-coaching people who come and work with us because alongside their skills, I look at what they love, and what they're made of – we bring them into the family.

Talent to me would be someone that really stands out, with a fresh approach that can remain focused. For events, students' extracurricular activities is what's impressive – they could have set up their own club night, or their own video channel or their own record label. But truthfully, I don't care about a degree. No-one senior in the events industry ever had one so I don't think it's actually that relevant. Sometimes it can even be a bit like "oh god, more event management students". The first event degree was only ten to fifteen years ago, before that nobody ever had one, and so how you ever got anywhere was through your personality skills. Whether you get a high first or a 2:1 isn't going to make a bit of difference. If you've set up your own business in your spare time, *that* will. We look for people who can make stuff happen.

It's also very much about working well with other people, and core skills such as, are you good with emails, are you reliable, what you can bring to the table? A degree alone just doesn't really cut it round here. That's not to say I don't think any kind of degree is a useful thing, but if someone did have one and they'd been running their own side projects, I'd be more interested.

One of the most talented people I know is a really young guy, he's about 19, left school at 16 because he just wanted to be a writer, and now he's one of the top VICE bloggers. He just left and got on with it and I have a lot of respect for that. I know that's not what events students perhaps want to hear but I always ask them "what do you learn? do they give you all the templates?" because for me that's really valuable, your budgets, your production schedules, your pre-production timeline, your labour sheet, your order list – spreadsheets are your life if you work in events.

When we talk about events themselves, you could basically define anything as an event and anything as an experience. But what's the difference between going to a club on a Saturday and going to, say, Slumber Rave? A place which looks like a gigantic bedroom with sprawling beds, strange mutated soft toys and everyone's in pyjamas having pillow fights. What's the difference? You're *definitely* going to have a really good time at one, that's for sure. You're going to go away thinking that's one of the best experiences you've ever had because it removed you, it had the power to peel away an outer layer that enabled people to go beyond their normal interactions.

What makes something an *experience* to me, is when the whole environment has been designed specifically to trigger some kind of reaction in the audience, even if that's just them feeling deeply comfortable or thinking "oh wow that's really innovative". It has to actively engage people and be something that resonates and provokes them to respond. It has to have a level of meaning beyond people congregating and talking and drinking. There's always going to be the human need to gather, and we can do that in a way where that's the only reason for it, or we can try to create another understanding of it, another depth of experience to it.

We react in certain ways according to the environment we are in, so if you change the environment, it encourages people to break free from their normal behaviour and interact in different ways. People are able to bond more because they have the chance and the freedom to be a slightly different person. They're in on the joke, they're allowed to express themselves and communicate with each other in perhaps ways they wouldn't usually, which comes from and adds to this unique experience. I mean it's basically the difference between a "meh" party and a really good party.

I'm an installation artist, so I may create a one-person walkthrough experience that's not an event, because there's no element of gathering. Is that a show or an event? I would say if people are there together, sharing information and bond, that's an event.

2002 was when I started as a producer of Lost Vagueness at Glastonbury. Back then, it was this muddy field with a burlesque casino vibe. It was a huge success and by 2005 the whole Victorian prohibition era trend had become massively popular. However by that time I was ready to evolve, so I set up my own company, Strong & Co, which is now 10 years old. Eventually Glasto wanted to move on from Lost Vagueness too, so in 2008 I ended up founding Shangri La with many of the same people but new ideas.

The first year, because we'd all been really restricted in this burlesque theme, we just needed to have a year where everyone shook out all their new ideas and did the crazy things that had been at the back of their minds for ages. But as a show it didn't actually work because it was too scattered, so I went back to the drawing board to pull everyone together under a central narrative. When you have that blank sheet of paper when you start an event, the first and foremost thought has to always be the audience. Who's it for and what do you want them to walk away feeling?

I realised there needed to be a theme that brings everyone together, something they can all respond to.

I had this field which was always dark and always raining, so I thought what would look good in that, that people would instantly recognise? Bladerunner. And so for the audience it became all about neon, fire, smoke, sex and music – an ultimate nihilistic pleasure city. The narrative was reflective of what I felt at the time, the promise of an ambrosial freedom that wasn't really free. Then the story evolved every year, and in 2012 the pleasure city was destroyed by its own hedonistic gluttony, and now it's in the end of a 4-year afterlife series. I stepped down from Shangri La after the 2015 show as I felt I'd achieved what I wanted to and it was in good hands to develop into the future. With Glastonbury I always felt more like a carer than an owner.

I think the proudest moment of my career was actually Shangri La in 2011, where I was like "now THIS is what I've been talking about since 2008!". That's where I'd wanted to get to, but sometimes getting it just right takes time. Especially because with Shangri La you only get one hit at it and you don't get to refine it with tight budgets and everything. It took that long to get all the clever people working together and to have all the right spokes in that wheel. And standing on that stage whilst everything was going off… It was just amazing.

Looking to the future, on one hand I think this industry will run off with more technology and Virtual Reality (VR). Right now I'm actually working on a massive tech installation for Twitter – an experimental exhibition where their agencies are guided through an installation which shows the variety of ways that artists and different people are using Twitter in innovative and creative ways. I want them to be seeing how it works, and how fundamental a tool Twitter is, and really feel its uniqueness.

Tech can make things infinitely more engaging, or at least less boring. The mind constantly seeks new and better experiences. But on the other side of that, I think there will also be a big shift toward the more authentic and human experience, because nobody wants to listen to, or engages with, branding messages anymore. Brands need to offer authentic, credible, tangible experiences, otherwise the message will never get through. So maybe we'll see a split in this industry.

Can these two things coexist? They very rarely do successfully, but I believe they can – it's just a case that the people with the big budgets for the VR and so forth are often working separately to the people who are making authentic experiences out of passion.

I'm excited by a future in which we combine powerful tech and comms with meaningful and authentic content.

THE

MAGIC

MOMENTS

CHRIS BARÉZ BROWN
FOUNDER, UPPING YOUR ELVIS

Events to me are a bit like weddings. There is a huge amount of pressure on them going beautifully and yet most of them are deeply forgettable.

I am talking particularly about when companies get large groups of people together for their annual sales conference, a new product launch, a quarterly review, some key messaging about the vision and how we are going to achieve it; the stuff that comes into our calendar and often makes our hearts sink.

These moments have the potential to be amazingly magical and yet most of the time they are wasted. Millions of pounds are flushed down the drain every year because people think about events in the wrong way. Yet, just like a wedding they can be unique, creative and special with a long-lasting impact. That is, as long as we don't follow the formulaic wedding plan delivering an experience that blends from one couple to another. Magnolia in hue.

This chapter sets out what I believe makes an event sing and guarantees that the moment is truly magical and memorable. Brace yourself and enjoy the ride!

GET CLEAR ON THE OBJECTIVE

All too often when you bring together lots of people, the opportunity to meld objectives becomes too great to bear. The CEO wants to review last year and get everyone excited about the next; the Marketing Director wants to talk about a new brand launch; the CFO wants to launch a new system for expenses and the Sales Director wants to talk about his amazing victories with one of the major grocers. HR have come up with some pretty good thinking on how to deliver against our development plans and the international team have got some very exciting news about a potential partnership in Bratislava.

Put this all together and all you have is noise.

The priority here is clarity. Get clear on exactly why you are getting together and what it is that you want to change as a result, ensuring you have singular focus in delivering it. Don't put things on the agenda just because they are nice to do or they fill time. And at all costs, avoid anything which could be deemed political. This is not a moment for 'divide and rule', it is a moment for 'unite'. The less you confuse people as to why they are there, the better the results.

If you go for multiple objectives there's a high chance you'll miss all of them.

If you go for one singular objective, there is a chance you will score.

THE EVENT STARTS BEFORE THE EVENT STARTS

As soon as you have the idea to get people together, it has begun. The way that you approach the planning and delivery will dictate how good it is. Create a tight team who really want to own it and invest time and energy in making sure they are committed to create a moment of legend. Forget what you have done before; we are starting with a shiny, new sheet.

Only have people on the team that can really add value and really want to be on it. Don't try and do this all yourselves, bring in external experts. They will bring you that extra pizzazz and hone an efficient moment machine.

When designing the flow make sure there is a clear story arc from beginning to end and remember that less is always more. Most designs are way too heavy and don't allow time for human interaction. Cut out 50% of your design and you've probably got it about right.

Every moment from the events inception can positively ladder up to its brilliance. The more you can do before the event to make sure that people are there in a positive frame of mind, the more chance of its success. Don't give people lots of homework to do, they won't thank you for it, but do get them to engage with what the event will deliver and why it is important to your organisation's success.

Use video as a way to make sure that people are positively primed and excited about turning up. Let them know that it's not about them being on the receiving end of thousands of

PowerPoints but it's about them as a team working together to create a shared output that will change the future forever.

QUALITY COUNTS

Don't allow anybody on stage unless they are good. Few leaders are confident enough to deliver well in front of large audiences so make sure whoever does, are well prepped and can nail their piece. Don't let senior leaders prep their pieces in isolation. Make sure this is a team effort where everyone comes together and supports each other in their delivery. One of the best events I have seen involved the senior leadership team spending three days together creatively developing the content and then practising delivering it to each other whilst getting live feedback. Never have I seen a tighter and more confident group of leaders who were committed to delivering something of wonder.

Small chunks of content are easier to digest and much easier to deliver, so don't have anybody doing pieces for more than 20 minutes unless they have worked on Broadway.

Make sure that all people involved in delivering material get to see the full picture and how their piece ladders up to deliver the overall objective and can support the event beyond just their piece.

Take the pressure off yourself by having a professional compere. They don't have to be expensive but they do need to be able to manage the energy and keep the linkages going so that story arc flows nicely.

WE ARE ONLY HUMAN

When considering the design, optimise the time people have together. There is no point investing in so many people getting there if all you do is talk at them. The value in bringing people together is the energetic and human experience that cannot be delivered by Skype. Make sure those moments are in your design.

For example, if you are launching agile working as a key cultural competence within the design, there needs to be some education about what that means and why it's important. Allow people to break out and process this new information so they understand what's in it for them and why they should change. You must give them a real experience as to what agile working looks like so they have an energetic memory and a positive emotion to go with this change. Offer them support so they know what happens next on a personal level to locking this change. Most importantly, all of this needs to be done in a fun, simple and human fashion.

IT'S ALL IN THE SET UP

Events work when standards are high. The key to success is making sure that you get the behaviours right for all attending. Make sure you have a clear set up to the event where you land the context and objectives: You get the energy right through some form of interaction and you are explicit about how you want people to be. Then ensure that you and your team role model those behaviours constantly. For example, if you don't want people using their mobile phones that means that everybody in the venue must do the same.

Get the venue right and avoid anything too corporate and dark. Natural light and opportunities to go outside are key to keeping our energetic state rocking. If we want people to feel captivated and inspired, we need to get them out of the cave.

Looking after people's energy is super important to keeping them engaged. One of the traps we often fall into is doing far too much, believing we should optimise the time we have together. It's much better to do less with full engagement than more with people drifting off. One consistent complaint from delegates of events is the lack of empathy with time and energy.

When people fly in from all around the world, planning in activities for every second of the day shows a certain insensitivity. Some of those worst moments are long and often alcoholic dinners where there is a pressure for everyone to be social, but actually all people want to do is go to bed. Make these things optional so that people choose what to do and can therefore make their activities fit with their energy levels. Never apply pressure to drink, it's just not cool. How many amazing events are ruined by people focusing more on the party than on the content? Hungover delegates are a sign that you got the design wrong; it's just plain embarrassing.

SHOWBUSINESS IS NO BUSINESS

Watch out for getting speakers that are there purely for entertainment. The event must certainly be entertaining and needs to have little treats scattered throughout but go for pure entertainment rather than pseudo-education.

Sure it's great to get fantastic speakers who keep people engaged and energised but there must be some learning that can be applied with real effect rather than just some funny stories and anecdotes being shared.

MIX IT UP

The design should make sure that for every hour of listening to stimulus there is an hour of processing it, pulling out key understandings and then generating output that drives a change in behaviour.

Whenever there is an opportunity for some breakout interaction, mix it up. We all have our favourite ways of keeping a group going but the key to staying on point is to go for variety.

If you have spent some time listening as an individual it's great to then process in pairs as you walk and talk outside of the room.

When you come back, if you share your big outtakes with another pair, once again the dynamic has changed and there is more of an opportunity to cross-fertilise.

Avoid doing too much in groups that are more than four. It's intimidating and only the loudest get heard. If you de-risk every interaction and make it one that all will be gently encouraged to partake in, then the whole thing becomes more productive.

Let them know just enough and then spike the plan with surprises. We all need a certain amount of information to be comfortable to show up and take part. That information involves objectives, timings, basic flow, what's needed from me, and little nuggets of fun. If you give them too much detail it leaves you little room for freedom; too little and they become nervous.

SURPRISE, SURPRISE!

Make sure that there are surprises throughout the design to spike the energy and keep them on their toes. Changing the dynamics and levels of participation are always winners; and any rock 'n' roll additions will never go amiss.

Whatever is your singular focus objective make sure it is ever present in all elements of design and delivery. People need to hear messages many times and in many contexts before they properly assimilate it. Don't be shy of banging it home many ways and many times.

The acid test of a good design is that when you look at it, you can't wait to attend. If all elements build to something bigger than their parts and take everyone on a journey that inevitably will deliver some value; you've done great work. Never turn up to event feeling uncomfortable about any element on the agenda. Your energy needs to be aligned and confident to make sure it really sings.

For optimum engagement, involve all the senses. People talking too much results in passive engagement, so keep changing it up. The more we do, the more we have to be present and the more we verbally process with each other the more conscious we will be throughout.

Don't make it too slick. The delivery should be human and simple and fun. When it's too slick we send out a message that to get on in this organisation you have to also be slick. This is an unfair and unreasonable expectation.

We best engage with people who are human; people who f*ck up and get things wrong. As long as we ride the bumps, things going wrong are endearing and connecting. Be yourself, mess up and you will be setting a clear expectation that people in your organisation can be themselves and nobody has to be perfect. In doing so you will get way more from your people. Authenticity brings brilliance. Don't pretend to be what you are not.

A wedding is memorable because something meaningful happens and happens in a way that is true to those getting married. Every detail is an articulation of what makes them unique and special: Therefore, there is resonance, joy and celebration throughout.

The best weddings are the ones where there is just enough planning done for people to relax and then when the curtain rises they just enjoy the moment rather than fret about the details. It's the same for an event. If you have fun and I mean genuine fun, so will everybody else.

And always end early. An extra 30 minutes just takes the pressure off and gives them a chance to slide out back to their busy lives without panicking about transport. How they leave is what they remember, get them leaving well.

They say planning a wedding is like running a company. You're the CEO of Love Inc. Keep this in mind when planning your moments and there will be no magnolia, just flashes of neon and an inspired, happy, shiny new team.

EVENTS – THE REAL SOCIAL MEDIA

SIMON BURTON
CEO, EXPOSURE COMMUNICATIONS

Events have proved remarkably robust and resilient as a communication medium. While every other medium has suffered declining audiences and revenues as a result of the digital revolution, face-to-face marketing has flourished. Whether B2B or B2C, live marketing and the power of in-person connection has found itself very much aligned with the digital age. It's not true for every event nor every market sector but overall "live" is very much living up to its name and kicking.

The digital revolution has created a whole new set of tools which have re-engineered broken business models, modernised outdated working methods and rethought how we conduct some of the most fundamental aspects of our day-to-day lives. Disruption and thinking the unthinkable are the orders of the day. Social media and the virtual world have co-opted the language of relationship – "connection", "like", "share", "recommend", "community" – and they add enormously to the process of relationship building, but the real manifestation of relationship will always be in the real world. In a world of screens, face-to-face has never been more powerful.

Why is that? What is it about events and the live experience that ensures an ever-growing slice of the marketing pie? The truth is one that event professionals realised long before the internet came along, but that the digital world has made abundantly clear to everyone. Human beings are social animals; every single one of our drives, desires and motivations is social. We exist and define ourselves at the most profound of levels through community and relationship to others.

We need to speak, to engage, to connect, to meet. Real relationships are more robust and meaningful than purely digital ones. There are two ways to make a connection, a digital "click" that's devoid of profound meaning or the genuine "click" that comes from the chemistry of meeting. People chemistry is a vital part of our business personalities and lives. Given an even choice, we'll always do business with people whose company we enjoy. Personality, presentation, energy and charisma count for a great deal in our personal and our brand's impact.

Research shows that over 90% of marketers and business directors believe that face-to-face marketing is the most effective media channel to convert prospects. But it's not just about closing the deal that gives face-to-face its power – relationships matter in business and all the evidence points to the same thing: face-to-face relationships last longer and have higher transactional values. Real-world relationships are longer lasting, better quality and worth more than relationships forged elsewhere. But that's obvious isn't it? Most of us would want to actually meet a potential partner from a dating site before we decide if we'd like to marry them.

Our world might be very different to that of our hunter-gatherer ancestors but we aren't very different to them.

Mutual interest, protection in a group, love, support, co-operation and celebration are things we do collectively. And one of the traits that marks us out most as humans is our need to gather round a real, or metaphorical, campfire and share stories. Stories which need an audience as much as they need an author. Events are the ultimate storytelling medium; many voices, diverse points of view, shared values deftly managed and leveraged to create a whole that is greater than the sum of its parts because stories, how we tell who we are, is the essence of every community. Not to mention the serendipity live often helps to create. You can't have a chance meeting if you're not there.

Would you rather be at a major sporting event your team wins or watch it on television? See your favourite band perform or pop the DVD in the player to see the concert? See someone else's cordon bleu meal on social media or savour the taste in the restaurant yourself? There is, quite simply, no substitute for being there. And the only thing better than being there is being there with people with whom you want to share the experience.

Brands, politicians, the media, all know and understand this. The moments of greatest emotional impact come from "being there" close to the epicentre of emotion. The point of connection and meaning is in the experience and the closer you can get your message to that beating heart of that experience the more it will resonate and connect with your audience.

Advertising slots in the Super Bowl aren't the most expensive simply because of the size of the audience, but because of the emotional punch the event itself carries and the fact that it is watched by the hearth – it's a collective shared experience that brands want to attach themselves to. The more people gathered around the screen to share the experience the greater its emotional resonance.

Even those political figures who have become adept at social and mainstream media campaigning put live events, touching their audiences directly, at the core of their campaigns. It's essential to connect, to communicate, to exchange ideas and make those ideas real and nothing does that as meaningfully and profoundly as an event. Face-to-face, eye-to-eye, handshakes and hugs are pretty poorly done in the virtual world.

Of course just because events are hardwired in our DNA, are part of what it means to be human, it doesn't necessarily follow that we are very good at them. Not everyone is a great storyteller or comedian, just as not everyone is a great athlete, or great hunter. Some of us are natural spectators rather than participants. Worse, in our highly developed and civilised world we've lost many of our natural attributes or rather we've had them "civilised" out of us.

Events are essentially a gathering of a group of strangers with shared interests; but since we've been told from an early age not to talk to strangers it can be difficult to start breaking down those barriers and get the conversation and connections going. This is more challenging in a B2B environment where we want the relationships forged to be commercial than it is in B2C environments like parties, weddings, and sporting events where our primary investment is emotional, but it's still true.

There's a challenge to the "human" component that makes events so great. They can expose our shyness, fears and prejudices. Great events and great event planners, however, mitigate these insecurities and fully utilise the power of events to communicate and harmonise. Seeing events as communication tools is a vital part of understanding this process. Too often it's the operational and logistical elements of events that are highlighted at the expense of the messaging and the communication impact.

The notion of "organising" does the event industry a huge disservice when competing against other media. Its focus on function rather than form denigrates the ability of events to create amazing aesthetics. Its focus on process rather than outcome obscures the way in which experiences generate real ROI. It suggests that events are brawn without brain and humping without heart. The event industry is finally starting to reposition itself as a serious part of the marketing mix not its poor subservient relation.

In fact, the relationship should always have starred events in the lead role. Events, with the exception of those modern innovations, pop-ups and flash mobs, are able to exploit every other part of the marketing mix to promote themselves. They are content machines, producing ideas, photographs, editorial, video and relationships as fundamental parts of what they do. Process is secondary. Events are all about outcome.

It's perhaps the notion of shared experiences which is the most exciting way in which social media seamlessly entwines with real-world events. Experiences now extend way beyond the physical walls that confine an event. Football matches, weddings, talent shows and political rallies are now amplified and commented upon by millions via social media. We're all journalists, we're all broadcasters and we're all media owners; and in the constant quest for compelling content, events and experiences are a powerful source of subject matter.

But great content isn't enough; great content needs powerful presentation, engaging storytelling and charismatic personality. If you're business is entirely "tech" and you're operating purely in a world of data then you might be able to avoid the need to connect and engage, but for most of us the ability to tell your story and make people want to listen is what sets us apart. In a world with information overload only the brightest, most appealing information stands a chance of being seen or heard.

Of course there is a downside to the emotional connection or "in the moment" feeling at an event. Events carry risk. When it goes wrong people's reaction and sentiment is emphasised in a negative way. Experiences are felt more keenly negatively as well as positively. No advertiser on a screen or paper ever actually saw or experienced the size of audience that they connected with, but an exhibitor in a trade show or brand conducting an experiential campaign is at the sharp end of the audience (present or not). Events are hard work, but they deliver measurable results.

Trade shows, as an example, are about as traditional and direct as marketing gets and the perfect launch pad for many an entrepreneurial endeavour or a young business wanting to get its product to market. Visitors attend exhibitions specifically to look for "new" stuff. So, in the case of that buyer who won't return your call or ignores your emails, he or she will be at the industry trade show on the hunt for the new, the innovative and the undiscovered and this gives you the perfect opportunity to put your product straight into their hands. But for every tale of great trade show success, there's one of wasted budgets and frustration at unmet targets. All too frequently the reasons for a lack of success are nothing to do with the show itself.

Here's a sobering stat to make you rethink all the clever plans and amazing graphics for your exhibition stand; 80% of the effectiveness of your exhibition stand is due to the stand staff. Forget about position in the hall or being next to the seminar theatre, the single most important component in exhibition success is your people. It's probably one of the most important factors in any context, but, face-to-face, great people make a great deal of difference.

And as if that stat wasn't sobering enough here's the kick into reality; 70% of trade show leads never get followed up. Never. Not even a generic email or brochure. Nothing. Nada. Zippity dooda. The hottest leads in the world are left to go icy cold.

And if it's true for exhibitions you can bet it's true for other event types. The best events require great people.

Events aren't an outlier. They aren't an anomaly. They don't have horizons that need to be extended. They exist, by their very nature, at the beating heart of communication. A consequence of a campaign, but also a necessary springboard for further communication and more profound relationship. Thank you notes and wedding photos, a children's party bag, watching the match highlights again on TV.

Because events exploit other channels to promote themselves they don't exist in isolation. There is no channel hopping, web surfing or newsagent's rack browsing for events. They must be promoted. Events aren't stumbled upon by chance. This has a very real consequence in terms of the opportunities to communicate and build audience around an event.

None of this is an "either or". Events aren't at war with digital. On the contrary, the best real-life event brands and people frequently have huge numbers of online connections and regularly share their real-life experiences online. Live plus digital is a very powerful cocktail. The basics of good business practice in the real world prevail in cyber space too. At their best the two work in tandem.

Whether or not you like the term amplification (I do like it, by the way) one of the greatest benefits social media has offered to events is to take amazing content beyond the four walls and time constraints of the physical event and share with like-minded people who aren't there. And "share" is the crucial world here. When we have great (or poor) experiences we want to let other people know about them. We want to spread the word and endorse our emotions. One of the golden rules for events and event marketing is this: If it's true for a major sporting or cultural event or a wedding then it's true in a diluted form for virtually every other type of event.

It's easy to forget in our digital world that the nature of human communication has always been social; the great moments of our lives have been shared in communities; and the "know who" of network has always been as important as the "know how". Social media is a fantastic enhancement to these basic human relationships but it is no replacement. People the world over have been shaking hands to greet one another and seal the deal for over 2,500 years. Over 90% of communication is non-verbal, so body language, tone of voice, personal presentation and environment are all more important in terms of meaning and understanding than any words exchanged.

Digital and social media in all their forms make things easier. Easier to follow up, easier to connect online, easier to share experiences and information and, from a sales and marketing ROI standpoint, easier to measure outcomes. Social networks and real-life meetings at their best co-exist and enhance one another. It's all about putting those components in the right order and recognising where priorities lie. And the priorities nearly always lie with people.

Some of social media's greatest successes are in the way it promotes and facilitates personal relationships. Want romance? Then dating sites will take you from an online picture to the love of your life. Want thousands of teenagers to come to a party at your house? Then publicise it on Facebook. Follow and engage with someone on Twitter and you can be certain that the conversation will flow more smoothly when you do meet. Profundity, durability and meaning in human relationships come from multiple connections in multiple environments with multiple touch points. The combination of real-life social events and digital world social media is a powerful cocktail to forge those relationships, make connections and share experiences.

THE TRADE SHOW MARKET

IN

SOUTHEAST ASIA

MARK COCHRANE

MANAGING DIRECTOR, BUSINESS
STRATEGIES GROUP, REGIONAL
MANAGER IN ASIA, UFI

EXECUTIVE SUMMARY

Southeast Asia has proven to be one of the most dynamic and vibrant trade fair markets in the world over the past three to five years. Growth, measured by net space sold, in the key Southeast Asian markets has consistently outperformed the rest of the region by a significant margin.

In 2014, the exhibition industry in Southeast Asia, yet again, performed strongly. Indonesia posted growth of net space sold of 9.2%, the Philippines – 8.8%, Thailand – 8.6%, Vietnam – 7.2% and Malaysia – 7.0%. Singapore was an exception posting growth of just 1.0% in 2014.[1]

This growth surge has been an ongoing trend. Southeast Asian markets also performed notably well during the five-year period 2010 to 2014. Singapore, Indonesia, the Philippines and Thailand all grew by well above the regional average, posting growth of between 27% and 33%. Malaysia and Vietnam grew in-line with the regional Asian average of 20%.

This growth is driven by a combination of factors including strong macroeconomic fundamentals, an improving portfolio

---

[1]	All figures in this chapter are drawn from the 2015 edition of the UFI-BSG report, "The Trade Fair Industry in Asia".

of available venues and supporting infrastructure as well as investment from international organisers in the form of launches, partnering with local players and acquisitions.

The size and structure of these markets varies widely and consequently, each one should be considered unique and separate – not taken as a whole. For example, in Thailand the growing trade fair market is centred in Bangkok where there are several world-class exhibition venues and a strong collection of international organisers operating, but at the same time the market is somewhat dominated by a government body which also acts as a major exhibition organiser. Contrastingly, in Singapore the government doesn't involve itself in the market as an event organiser and instead actively supports the industry through policies and financial incentives, but the market in Singapore is decidedly a more mature market with lower growth prospects.

This chapter provides a brief summary of the key Southeast Asian trade fair markets on a country-by-country basis highlighting the role of government, the quality of venues and supporting infrastructure, the structure of the market and the overall outlook for the industry in each country. Despite notable challenges in many of these markets, the trade fair industry's growth prospects in Southeast Asia remain undoubtedly exciting and substantial.

THAILAND

The trade fair market in Thailand is easily the largest in Southeast Asia with more than 550,000 net sq^m sold in 2014. (The second largest market, Singapore, recorded net space sales of 332,000 sq^m in the same period.)

Thailand is also the most resilient trade fair market in the region. In the past five years, the Thai trade fair industry has faced crisis after crisis: a military coup, political unrest, floods as well as violent protests. Despite all of this, the trade fair market in Thailand has repeatedly posted solid growth – year after year.

In terms of net space sold, the Thai market grew by well over 8% in 2014 and by 27% in the past five years (2014 vs. 2010). There is plenty to recommend the market in Thailand. With an export-oriented economy featuring a GDP of approximately US$375 billion and population of nearly 70 million, the fundamental pieces clearly are all in place.

The key trade fair market, Bangkok, has a strongly developed infrastructure including two world-class, privately owned venues – IMPACT (137,000 sq^m) and BITEC (36,000 sq^m). In addition, BITEC has an expansion plan underway which will lift its capacity to 70,000 sq^m by the end of 2016.

The country has aspirations to build a trade fair industry that serves the ASEAN region, but the core of events in Bangkok successfully serve its sizable domestic market as well as a significant number of international buyers – to a lesser or greater degree depending on the event category.

The Thai government is strongly supportive of trade fairs through the well-funded and active Thailand Convention & Exhibition Bureau (TCEB), but at the same time, another branch of government, the Department of International Trade Promotion (DITP) is in fact the largest exhibition organiser in Thailand. The DITP's role as both a government body and event organiser is an impediment to commercial growth as DITP's events cover some of the most attractive trade fair topics.

Despite the role of the DIPT, the trade fair market in Thailand is a dynamic and reasonably commercial one with strong local players and many international organisers such as UBM, Reed, AllWorld and Diversified. In addition, Bangkok is somewhat unique in Asia in that its leading venues are privately owned and operated (IMPACT and BITEC).

Economic growth in Southeast Asia is forecast to remain quite strong. Given that as well as the trade boost that is expected from the ASEAN Economic Community (a new free trade zone), the trade fair industry in Thailand should continue to expand and grow. Space constraints in Bangkok are minimal and venues in secondary markets such as Chiang Mai and Pattaya will provide opportunities for niche, regional topics.

MALAYSIA

In terms of net space sold, the trade fair market in Malaysia is quite large (321,000 sq^m), but the potential upside remains significant. With a population of more than 30 million and its GDP approaching US$330 billion, there is plenty of room for launching new trade fairs.

In recent years, Malaysia's net space sold has grown rapidly. In 2014, space sold was up 7%. Over the past five years, net space sold in Malaysia jumped by more than 21%. This growth did not go unnoticed by the international organisers as a number of local events and organisers have been acquired. UBM Asia, ITE Group and Sphere Exhibits have all acquired Malaysian events in recent years. At this point, most of the leading international players have well-established portfolios in Malaysia – including Reed, UBM Asia, ITE Group and Allworld to name a few.

There are positives in the Malaysian trade fair market including the potential size of the market, the relative openness of the market and the support for the industry through the Malaysian Convention and Exhibition Bureau (MyCEB). The key issue is the clear need for additional venue capacity – particularly in Kuala Lumpur, the centre of Malaysia's trade fair industry.

The Kuala Lumpur Convention Centre and Putra World Trade Centre both offer approximately 10,000 sq^m of gross indoor space. The largest venue, Malaysia International Exhibition & Convention Centre (MINES), is 38,000 sq^m, but it is more than 20km outside the city centre.

There are plans to build a new venue, MITEC, that will add nearly 50,000 sq^m to the market, but that venue won't open until at least 2017 – possibly later. Until the venue capacity issue is adequately addressed, many of the key organisers (both local and international) maintain that they are not able to fully realise potential of the Malaysian market.

SINGAPORE

Singapore is one of the most mature trade fair markets in Asia. It has a world-class portfolio of venues and supporting infrastructure, a well-funded, supportive government and a strong, professional collection of organisers.

Net space sold has increased more than 33% since the opening of the Marina Bay Sands venue in 2010, rising from about 250,000 sq^m to over 332,000 sq^m in 2014. It is worth noting, however, that growth of space sales has slowed, rising just 1.0% in 2014 – the slowest growth rate in the region. Many key international organisers maintain operations here including Koelnmesse, Messe Düsseldorf, Reed Exhibitions, AllWorld, ITE Group and UBM Asia.

It would be difficult to fault Singapore's infrastructure. In terms of venues, there is Singex (100,000 sq^m), Marina Bay Sands (41,000 sq^m) and Suntec (nearly 39,000 sq^m). In addition, the supporting logistical infrastructure from immigration to customs to hotels to service providers, is done to the highest standard.

However, as a mature, developed market, the medium-term outlook for the industry in Singapore is consistently modest growth. Increases of 2% to 4% should be anticipated in the next three to five years. Although Singapore has all of the key pieces in place, the market is relatively small with a population of about 5.5 million. While the larger, industrial trade fairs are thriving in Jakarta, Bangkok and Kuala Lumpur, Singapore will need to focus on smaller, niche events that cover service and creative industries instead.

INDONESIA

Despite a recent surge in space sold, Indonesia remains one of the most underserved trade fair markets in Asia. Net space sold in Indonesia increased by 9.2% in 2014, topping the strong 7.0% growth recorded in 2013. Indonesia has been posting similarly rapid growth rates for the past five years. Overall, net space sold increased from 167,750 m² in 2010 to 221,750 m² in 2014. That is a 32% increase – one of the highest in the region.

On top of this, Indonesia's economy looks to remain strong. GDP growth of 5.0% to 5.5% is forecast for the next two years. Add to this a population of over 250 million and a GDP of close to US$890 billion – and Indonesia's trade fair industry is well positioned for further expansion. The establishment of the ASEAN Economic Community (AEC) in late 2015 will likely stimulate incremental economic growth as Indonesia's key trading partners in the ASEAN countries lower tariffs.

These positive factors have been bolstered by recent improvements to Indonesia's infrastructure. Jakarta's venue capacity received a vital boost in 2015 with the opening of the Indonesia Convention Exhibition Centre (ICE), which added 50,000 m² to the market. ICE is managed by Deutsche Messe and should serve to unlock significant space sales growth in the coming three to five years.

With all of these positive indicators, it is not a surprise that international players have been combing the market for potential partners and acquisitions. Reed, Tarsus, UBM and ITE Group have all inked deals in recent years. The size of the market as well as the absence of government interference (as an organiser) in the market has driven much of this enthusiasm.

This, combined with the significant boost in Jakarta's capacity as well as forecasts for robust economic growth, will all serve to spur net space sales in Indonesia into the high single digits (7% to 9%) in the coming three to five years.

VIETNAM

Vietnam stands as what seems like a missed opportunity. A lack of investment in venues and infrastructure is continually preventing the unlocking of significant growth in this market. The largest exhibition venue in the country is less than 10,000 m² and there are no announced plans to increase capacity in the coming years. Other challenges include red tape, unnecessary bureaucracy and a lack of a critical mass amongst local organisers.

As a result of these issues, international organisers have paid little attention to this market in recent years. There are a few exceptions. Hong Kong-based organisers CP Exhibition and Adsale Exhibitions as well as UBM Asia have small-scale events in Vietnam, but clearly the potential for the market is far greater.

Despite this, net space sold in Vietnam in 2014 grew by 7.2% – albeit from a very small base. This growth was, nonetheless, ahead of the Asian average of 6.8%. Space sold increased from 158,750 m² in 2013 to almost 170,250 m² in 2014. Over the past five years, the market in Vietnam grew roughly in-line with the regional average, with net space sold increasing by 20.3% between 2010 and 2014.

Vietnam hosted 58 trade fairs in 2014 which generated estimated revenues of US$50 million. Vietnam is another example of an underserved exhibition market with large potential upside. The country has a population of 91 million and a US$186 billion economy that has consistently posted GDP growth of approximately 5% or more. Despite this obvious potential, Vietnam's market remains smaller than that of the small city of Macau.

Net space sales growth of 3% to 5% over the next two to three years is a best-case scenario and with the venue and supporting infrastructure being what it is, there is little to no expectation for the market to surpass this. Without a game-changing event such as the construction of a new, reasonably-sized venue or increased government attention and support for the industry, Vietnam will remain essentially an untapped market.

PHILIPPINES

It has been encouraging in recent years to watch the Philippines garner increased attention from international organisers. That said, the underlying challenges holding back the market remain firmly in place.

The market, in terms of net space sold is small. In 2014, space sold in the Philippines increased 8.8%, rising to more than 164,500 m^2 – up from 151,250 m^2 in 2013. The Philippines was also a strong performer during the past five years as net space sold increased from 128,250 m^2 to 164,500 m^2, representing growth of more than 28% – well above the regional average of 20%.

Even after this recent burst of growth, the Philippines remains the second smallest market in Asia – only ahead of Pakistan. In 2014, the Philippines hosted just 46 trade fairs with an average size of 3,576 m^2 – far below the regional average of 8,644 m². In terms of revenues, the market is also the second smallest in the region – at US$27 million in 2014.

Its sizable economy (GDP of US$280 billion) and its population nearing 100 million suggest an obvious opportunity for growth. Along with Indonesia and Vietnam, the Philippines stands as one of the most underserved trade fair markets in Asia.

This is changing as international organisers have recognised the potential in Manila and beyond, and have moved to partner and launch new shows throughout the country. UBM Asia, Comexposium and others have partnered and launched events in the Philippines in the past two to three years. This should serve to professionalise the industry and spur on growth.

Unfortunately, the largest exhibition venue in Manila offers a capacity of less than 10,000 m². A new venue with a capacity of 30,000 m² to 40,000 m² would definitely unlock pent-up growth and attract even more international organisers. It comes down to the usual set of requirements: investment in supporting infrastructure, larger venues and more effective government support of the trade fair industry are all required to enable the market in the Philippines to move forward.

OTHER SOUTHEAST ASIAN MARKETS

The trade fair markets in Myanmar, Laos and Cambodia are nascent. There is, of course, good potential in all three of these markets, but currently there are several factors stacked against development of the trade fair industry there.

Unsurprisingly, the venue and supporting infrastructure is underdeveloped. Government awareness of the trade fair industry is absent. There are few local organisers operating in these markets and finally, there are significant bureaucratic challenges to setting-up and operating a business in Myanmar, Cambodia and Laos.

There are positive signs of improvement – particularly in Myanmar where the military rulers have stepped back and opened the market to increased international trade and business. Myanmar's hotel and supporting infrastructure is improving. A Thai company has built a small, semi-permanent, tent-style venue and international organisers such as AllWorld, ITE Group and UBM have all experimented with small-scale conferences and exhibitions.

In short, these three markets are difficult, but promising. Each represents a case of "watch this space".

WHY EVENTS ARE A MORE EFFECTIVE TOOL TO SUPPORT BRANDS

NICK DE BOIS

CHAIRMAN,
UK EVENTS INDUSTRY BOARD

BACKGROUND

I am currently Chairman of the UK Event Industry Board, a new board put together to enable the events industry to work closer with government and to give the sector a voice at the policy-making table. The role was offered to me because of my experience within the events industry as a business owner, my work supporting the industry as an MP, as well as my work with UKTI, BIS and other government agencies that care about the expansion of business in the UK.

The board acts in an advisory capacity with two clear objectives. Firstly, in partnership with the events industry we're looking to identify and recommend key events that Britain should be hosting; both that will help grow and support the events sector and that will drive forward the UK's industrial strategy. Once these events have been identified, we utilise the power of government to help support the events community to pitch and win the targeted events (something other countries do much more effectively than the UK).

Secondly, we are looking across the industry at UK events that already exist and that, with some help, could, should they wish to be, become flagship events; attracting greater interest and support from overseas.

The rationale behind the board is that if we can start to win events that are currently held elsewhere in the world, then that not only brings some of the brightest minds and biggest companies into the UK, but we have the opportunity to showcase what Britain can offer on a long-term basis. What can be a win for the events sector can also be a win for the wider UK economy.

The Events Industry Board is also there to identify and break down the barriers for Britain to become the most competitive destination in the world. We're not there yet, but we're on our way. I spent five years as a Member of Parliament in which I chaired the All-Party Parliamentary Group (APPG) on the UK events industry, which produced the first parliamentary inquiry into the competitiveness of the UK as a destination of choice. It is good to see the Government responding to those recommendations with the event sector's active support.

It's not always obvious to every government minister or indeed the wider public who get to watch the spectacle of something like the Olympics that there's actually an extraordinary multi-billion pound industry behind it; an industry that employs well over half a million people across the country. One of our great challenges now is not to let the 2012 Olympics be the peak of the UK events industry, but indeed see it as the catalyst to have spurred the industry onto greater things; not necessarily through events with such a high profile, but certainly through those with a similar value to the UK, of which the business-to-business events and exhibition sector are a major contributor.

For over 25 years I have worked within and alongside this exciting industry; having founded and run Rapiergroup, worked in the APPG for events and now within the Events Industry Board. After five years in Parliament, what now gets me out of bed every day is how can we make the events sector even better by influencing government policy to help, not hinder, the sector, and ensure the industry's success is also to the wider benefit of the UK.

THE CHALLENGES FACING THE INDUSTRY

I like to think of events as essentially bringing people with a common interest together on a shared, live platform. The temptation for some in this digital age is to think that gathering "in person" isn't that important, but I disagree. The events industry is all about bringing people together, it's about getting customers talking, and about using a multitude of different platforms right across the sector to achieve that.

How to be most effective in doing that is something that challenges us every day, as both providers and their clients seek competitor advantage.

When I traditionally think about events, I think of companies bringing together their employees, agents or customers, from around the world into conference rooms, ballrooms and exhibition floors. They'll all get together and watch fantastic videos, listen to empowering speakers and engage in stimulating conversations between delegates; that can be a very powerful motivator. However, the sector is now challenging itself as to whether this is enough. It's right to do so as well because like so many marketing activities, the money spent on events is coming under even greater scrutiny every day.

The current debate is around how the sector should be moving towards advocating "experiential" event solutions. Although the concept is not particularly new, it is an idea whose time may have come. Definitions will vary as to what precisely experiential is, but broadly speaking it's safe to explain that where an event is essentially one person talking to say 1000 delegates, by contrast experiential is where you're effectively holding multiple conversations with individuals at one event through an "experiential" creative event solution.

Now clearly that doesn't mean one person is going around talking to each individual person, but the whole creative treatment will be designed to give each person that intimacy of experience. At the former more conventional event I first referred to, the "take out" for the visitor is going to be pretty similar for most people in attendance. But if you go into an experiential event, you're more likely to feel as though the experience has been tailored directly to you and the messaging more effective if that's the case.

Yet, from a business point of view, all this could be all meaningless if it does not deliver for the customer what he wants.

THE VOICE OF THE CUSTOMER

My experience is that from the customer perspective, the important issue is that an event must result in a transaction. I think sometimes in this industry we can get so wrapped up talking about experimental or alternative ideas that we risk losing sight of the fact that the event is only really there to do one job; and that is to help move the client business forward, and primarily that means driving sales.

I remember a very senior director of a plc once saying to me at the end of a really long and intense presentation, "… but is this going to help me sell? That's all I want to know." We have to remember that.

And given that we have to pitch ourselves now against all the other substantive marketing tools that are at the disposal of the customer, the case has to be made for the best route to that transaction. Therefore, we must make the case as to why the events sector is more powerful or more appropriate than advertising, sales promotion or social media; or at the very least why, as part of an integrated marketing mix, the event increases the prospect of a successful transaction.

Our goal is to fight the corner for why events are a more effective tool to support brands, their goals and sales; which will do more to support the longevity of the sector by establishing value at the boardroom table. I don't think we've quite done that yet in this industry. We're getting there, and we're doing a lot more work, but that's where we need to take ourselves.

In a way we've been a bit slow to this. Whenever you buy something, it's partly though emotion and partly logic. The only thing that differs is the ratio between those two. I think the ability events have to drive emotional engagement and turn that into a transaction is phenomenal. It's something I think marketers have always been looking for but have relied heavily on other media to deliver. If you look at good advertising, it's moving you emotionally by relying on sound and imagery to stimulate you, but it has nowhere else to go once the ad has run. The live events sector has a huge advantage in that it can utilise every sense to deliver both a powerful, emotional message on a shared platform with the customer; which is a short step away from concluding the transaction.

Can we get there? I'm actually very positive that we continue to be extremely well placed to continue to see significant growth in the maturity and the quality of what we do.

THE FUTURE

A word of warning; we must be careful that we don't just have a conversation with ourselves. We must also have this dialogue with the end user, be that a business, a customer, a tourist visitor or a business visitor that comes through conferences or delegations.

We must be careful not to go right up our own backsides and come out feeling good about ourselves without having actually convinced anyone of the merits of our industry. This is the crucial message. We're at a great stage because we've got people's attention; we've got the Secretary of State for the Department for Culture, Media & Sport; we've got the Prime Minister's attention, and we've got the industry hungry to do better things for itself. But now we've got to use this opportunity to make sure we can make the case to the people who matter – businesses, their customers, their clients and their shareholders – essentially, the end users.

I think part of the beauty of this industry and what we do is that every event is a prototype. It doesn't matter how much experience you have in logistics, design or delivery; every one is a prototype. A live event is going to open with or without you being ready and every one brings its own challenges. In a way I think that's the wonderful mystery of what we do – we don't know exactly what's going to happen and yet we have the beauty of knowing in the space of six months or a year, what we started with on paper is going to come to fruition before our eyes.

In some ways, when I first started I wish I'd been able to appreciate the power of what we do rather than fear it, which is what I did. I used to almost go into events on a negative, seeing it as this huge list of things to dread going wrong. I wish I'd had that confidence and understanding of what we could do, but we've grown up and we've become much more mature and confident as an industry.

I also remember always being conscious, as far back as 1989, that we were at the dud end of the marketing mix and I knew that exhibitions were always looked down upon by the more sophisticated players in marketing. But now that has changed dramatically and we're much more respected for the complexity of what we do, and the vast range of skills we possess.

But this is a rapidly growing and evolving industry, and whether we can recruit the kinds of people to deliver the skills that we need is another question. I think our current skill base in the UK is limited, and I don't think we have the sufficient skills in this country to support the aspirations of what we want to do and where we want to go. The answer to this lies in the hands of the industry. We should be taking much more of a proactive role in working with colleges and universities to help create and shape courses and degrees that will help support the industry as it evolves and to fulfill its needs. If we shape up, we could create very effective apprenticeships that would help mould and train people with the skill sets that we need.

But to my mind, a qualification is not necessarily essential. It's terrific if you are innovative, articulate and you have a sense of discipline, but what I would say about our sector is that if you have that entrepreneurial flair, through mentoring and guidance, you will thrive in this industry. One that I think is one of the most attractive, exciting and fulfilling sectors to set up and run your own business in. If I met someone who was at a live event and I could see that they just had that real buzz for it, that can make up for many other shortcomings. Because aptitude you can teach, but a genuine passion and love for what you do is something you're born with.

IN CONCLUSION

The events industry is looking up and out; something we've not done for a long time and that we're learning to do as we go. My advice to the industry is now to listen as well; there are strong messages from government but even stronger ones from business that can make us more respected, appreciated and procurable.

If we don't listen or we listen and don't act we'll quickly grow old and out of favour. We've had the platform to shout our value and to tell our story; now is the time for true engagement and collaboration.

WORK HARD, PLAY HARD

AND

Be Kind

SEAN DOYLE
DIRECTOR OF BRAND AND
CREATIVE, CLIVE

I first found myself in the events industry during a planned year off between college and university.

I began working in a proactive sales role for a large catering company, but at just 18 years old I knew very little about the industry, and was literally handed the Yellow Pages and tasked with cold-calling companies to speak to their marketing and sales directors about how they entertained their clients. I guess I was a bit of an odd fit for the role but I did enjoy the conversations and trying to work out what event or hospitality was right for this company's client. It was there that I worked out pretty early on that I wanted to be in a position to create events that were right for audiences rather than find clients to buy pre-defined packages.

I remember being in awe of the big creative events I'd see in the industry magazines and from there I moved to London to seek a more creative, hands-on role. I ended up getting an event executive role in a very small boutique agency that specialised in celebratory and team-building events. I managed to take my first enquiry on day two and by day five had already done site visits and booked the event. I remember my colleague talking me through a list of upgrades to discuss with the client and I loved that consultative approach of working out how she wanted her guests to feel, what entertainment and what look and feel was right for them.

I stayed with that agency for nearly five years, but by the time I'd worked my way up to Head of Creative I knew events could do more than just entertain, and I was keen to learn more. I was fascinated by content-led events and working internationally on much bigger productions so I accepted a more junior role of Account Manager at Concerto Live, now known as Clive, of which I currently stand as Director of Brand and Creative.

In the last eight years I've had the chance to work with big brands like Facebook, Virgin, Instagram and BT on both live and digital projects in about 20 different countries. I worked my way through Sales & Marketing Manager, then Head of Creative Services, building the sales, creative and digital teams, and most recently we bought out the remaining Concerto Group shares and rebranded to Clive (an abbreviation of Communicate Live), a fully independent agency. I was appointed to the board of directors in May 2016.

I don't think I'd change anything about my journey through this industry, but one thing I'm glad I realised early on was it's all about meeting people, networking and experiencing new locations and suppliers for events in person, rather than through directories or internet searches. I was out at networking events nearly every night of the week in the early stages of my career, making some great industry relationships and I knew of every event space or unusual supplier. My colleagues would jokingly refer to me as a 'walking, talking encyclopedia of the industry' but it was being able to reel these off at a drop of a hat that showed clients I knew my stuff, and that I could bring something to their event that they couldn't bring themselves.

That would be my recommendation to someone starting out; get out there, meet people, see places, experience everything you can and throw yourself into the industry. It's definitely something a lot of people do less as they get older or when they feel they've seen it all before, so it's a great way of making yourself invaluable to your team and clients by being in the know!

In the Clive studio we have a print up which says 'Work Hard, Play Hard and Be Kind', which, from my own experience I feel embodies this industry pretty well. It's definitely hard work, with shorter and shorter lead times and really big asks in pitch scenarios where you're often one of perhaps six agencies putting weeks of work into what is sometimes a speculative brief. You need to be a social person that's for sure – there's always a new destination, venue, piece of technology, entertainment or speaker to see, so you need to be social and out and about a lot to keep up. And finally, this is a people business and success is built on relationships and recommendations.

To us, an event is something that takes place. It's a happening that you invite people to come along and witness, but not in the same way as if they were part of an *experience*. An experience does more than just let people be fed and watered whilst you tell them something. An experience is about letting an audience *discover* something. It usually involves engaging more than just a few senses and if done right should mean your audience have a much longer-lasting impression of your brand or message, and are much more likely to take some kind of action. That could be to tell more people about your product, to advocate it on social media or to spend more money with you. That's because an experience means they should go away thinking 'I feel this about that brand' rather than 'I was told this about that brand'.

When we start to plan an event, the first question is always 'Where do we want to get to?', so I guess you could say we start at the end first. Once that's clear, we need to go back to the beginning to work out exactly where we're starting from. Because when you know those two things, planning the journey between the two should be a lot easier. When it comes to every element of the event, from venue, to theme, to speaker, food, activity you can ask yourself 'Will this decision affect how my audience feels?', 'Will it help my audience get from where they are now, to where we want them to be?'

I believe success always starts with working out what you want your audience to do as a result of taking part in your event or experience – what do you want them to think and feel? Also, if a client allows you access to delegates to measure their understanding and feelings before an event, then you're much more likely to have a successful event, because you know where you're starting from. Sometimes clients don't want to ask too many questions, they feel their guests are too busy or won't want to disclose too much information, but we find they're often more than happy to share how they feel about something and what they want to know. Knowing the event is designed to address their needs increases attendance and improves the experience for everyone. It also means you can really measure the success afterwards by talking to the audience again to gauge uplift in understanding and feelings.

However, when planning an event it's essential to always consider the needs of the stakeholders. You must work together to reach an understanding about the point of the event and the action you want the audience to take in the first place. Once you have that clear direction, you should be able to convince the stakeholders to consider the audiences needs in every element of the event. For example, for a hospitality event, the end goal might be for a group of clients to feel valued and appreciated. There might be a temptation to look at hosting the event in the coolest new warehouse or pop-up that just so happens to be in an up-and-coming part of town, but realistically you need to think about the client's journey from start to finish. Where do they work? Where do they live? How are they going to get to the venue and back to the mainline station again afterwards? If you end up asking your guest to spend an hour travelling across town using tubes and buses or spend £50 on a taxi, all of these things will contribute to how the guest feels about your event, your hospitality and in turn your company. Looking at the bigger picture, is there somewhere more convenient but equally as good quality that you could select and show the audience you have considered their needs? Or if not, how can you simplify the process for them?

At the heart of it, a successful experience is all about engagement; a majority of people saying 'I now have a clearer vision of the aims and goals for the future of the business and the part I play' or 'I feel really valued by my employer after that amazing trip and I'm going to do everything I can to exceed my targets again next year to ensure my place on the next trip'. That to me shows that you have engaged with someone. Equally, someone spending the time to advocate the experience by posting a great photo, video or positive message about the experience on social media – that's engagement too because the person has taken the decision to want to be associated with your brand publicly. They thought 'That was unusual, impressive and the kind of thing I want people in my network to associate me with'.

One of the most memorable and engaging events I ever attended was actually Bestival, the music festival on the Isle of Wight by Rob da Bank. I know it's not a brand experience itself but actually that's what drew me to it. I'd been to lots of festivals that had big name sponsors and had always had a great time, but the first time I went to Bestival back in 2006, I remember feeling that all of the previous festivals I'd been to had felt soulless and corporate in comparison. Everything at Bestival had been created by Josie da Bank, the Creative Director and Producer, and all felt so well thought-out. She had a real vision for the event and the way she wanted guests to feel. Everything from the hand-painted signage to the dressing of the walkways, carefully curated sideshow entertainment, the sights, smells and sounds made you feel this was more than just a commercial event. There were zones and sculptures to explore and activities to take part in but none of them were brand experiences, just part of the infrastructure designed to enhance the festival-goers experience. I know a lot of festivals do this really well now, but I think Bestival was one of the first. Whilst I'm not saying I wish I could create a consumer music festival, I do remember wanting to bring all of those small touch points, details, discovery and ways of engaging the senses to brand events, as a way of making them feel more authentic and less like a hard corporate sell.

Without a doubt, the biggest change I've noticed throughout my time in the events industry is the rise of experiential events. There are activities and activations popping up at music festivals, shopping malls, train stations and high streets from brands desperate to get some real engagement with their audience. Letting their customers get their hands on a product, engage their senses and make them feel something about the brand. That's well and truly crossed over into the B2B world now too – clients now see the value in offering a unique brand experience to set themselves apart from the competition. Even the corporates aspire to be like the coolest consumer brands out there.

For example, we recently did a conference for an automotive client. They wanted to really surprise and delight their employees and also make the whole thing a bit more experiential. They're used to inviting all their people to the annual conference at the same time at the same place, which is actually not great for their business, having all 400 employees away from desks and phones in one room. So we started solving their problems by splitting them into smaller groups, and essentially we bought them in for a pretty basic keynote conference, but after 15 minutes the curtain dropped behind the speaker onstage and we invited the audience up onto the stage to find three different zones to experience a day in the life of their customer. One environment was the home, with a full set design and actors and all the classic distractions going on in the background like the TV blaring, and it was for them to understand the experience the customer would be having when they speak to them on the phone, and why perhaps they wouldn't be interested in speaking to them at that time. So there are very simple and effective ways to incorporate experiential into B2B scenarios; it's about moving people around, getting their hands on things and bringing their messages to life. And bringing a bit of theatre into it is a great way to do that.

I think at this point I'd compare the events industry to a younger version of the advertising industry. It's a growing and increasingly respected part of the marketing mix, but what the advertising industry did years ago was to stop working for free and create a standard practice of agencies working on retainers. I think it's happening more often in the event industry and certainly something I've noticed that clients in the US expect but not so much in the UK right now. I do think if our industry could get to the same place as the advertising industry then it would likely command some more respect as a really skilled marketing resource but it's likely we as an industry need to work on the whole ROI model, justification of budget and proof of engagement before we can really get to this stage.

Moving toward the future, measurement definitely needs to be a focus, and finding a way to prove the worth of an event by a change in feeling or behaviour. I think the use of VR technology will move on from just showcasing ideas, gaming and possible products to connecting actual people around the world so you can genuinely feel like you're in the same room as colleagues when having a meeting, when you might be the other side of the world. In 50 years we'll probably all be 3D printing our own perfect venues and offering trips to the moon as sales incentives. But in all seriousness, the power of human interaction and real face-time with your staff and customers will probably become even more valuable as our lives get even busier, noisier and even more bogged down with technology.

THE IMPOSSIBLE IS POSSIBLE

IN THE EVENTS INDUSTRY

TRACY HALLIWELL
DIRECTOR OF BUSINESS
TOURISM AND MAJOR EVENTS,
LONDON & PARTNERS

Events isn't all about party planning, weddings and festivals – there are a multitude of drier events, and a lot of business and strategic planning behind the scenes. My advice to event students is that it's a fun industry, but be prepared for hard work.

I've been Director of Business Tourism and Major Events for London for ten years now, and I'd say this is certainly a rollercoaster industry. It is full of incredibly high moments, it's exhilarating, it's a lot of fun, you can do all the great things like travelling and experience some of the most amazing things in the world, however at the same time it's not as glamorous as it sounds. There's a lot of hard work to it, but the results do pay off and you do get to experience an awful lot that you perhaps wouldn't otherwise. If there was something I wish I'd known at the start of this journey, it would probably be that rules can and most likely will be bent or completely rewritten. You can get a brief and at the first reading you might think "that's completely impossible", but the impossible is the possible in the events industry because you can make anything happen, sometimes you just have to think outside the box.

If you're looking for the difference between an event and an experience, at the root of it all I'd say an event itself is a fairly passive engagement; it's turning up and participating, there's probably a lot of speaker sessions, some note-taking and a chance of networking. An experience is more of an immersive engagement you actually get involved in, and you walk away having experienced something new, something engaging which sparks your attention and your longer-term retention of the moment.

When beginning to plan a new event, it's always important to go back to the beginning and ask 'Why are we doing this event? What's the outcome we want to get? Who's the audience going to be?' And only once you're sure about the answers to those questions, can you start on the logistical things – such as where are we going to host it? Location is a big attractor as to why people attend some events, so it's got to have a wow factor, and needs to embrace both the practical, logistical needs as well as the emotional needs of the audience. Cost is always going to factor into the planning too, but start with the What, How and Why.

The right brief is also about understanding what your senior stakeholders want. They're the paymasters at the end of the day so they've got to be satisfied that their event has achieved the right outcomes for them. But at the same time, if you're not delivering what your audience is going to be interested in, then that's not going to achieve their outcomes anyway. Finding the balance is the difficult part because it's having to weigh up what are the most important things to achieve out of a long list, how many of those you can deliver to the best of your ability, and how many you can touch upon, because you might not able to do them all, but try to find a win-win solution.

Something we've been doing quite a lot of research on recently is the event logistics versus the event experience, and oftentimes as event planners we spend so much time on the former, we fall down on the latter. Going back to audience engagement, whilst the event needs to work it's so much more powerful if you can touch the emotional side of people, so we're beginning to think about things like the look and feel of the venue, what smells are around and what music is going to play. The event has got to play to all the different senses to enhance the experience. There's been a lot of work recently on sensory perceptions and how that can make a good event versus a bad event. These are all the things we're starting to incorporate into great event planning.

The best event I have ever attended has to be the 2012 London Olympic & Paralympic Games, which was just phenomenal. I think we well and truly banished that whole perception that the Brits were stuffy and boring and didn't have a sense of humour. I was actually lucky enough to do two outstanding events during the Olympics; the first being the men's 100m final and just being in that stadium with the excitement of the Great British public was incredible, and the second was the Paralympic cycling. That was an intensely emotional experience because the velodrome is an extraordinary but quite small venue, so you're right there around the track, and to witness these amazing Paralympians who are almost at the same power as the able-bodied was just incredible. Being a part of that was one of my proudest moments in my career, perhaps only seconded by being awarded the MBE for Business Tourism in 2014. But maybe that was just because I could take my mum.

Another early event that sticks in my mind is seeing the Blue Man Group about twenty years ago in Las Vegas. It was the first immersive theatre show I'd been to which really brought the audience into the show – the Slava Snowshow is a similar experience. I'd never been to anything quite like that before, and whilst not strictly an event, we have learnt a lot from theatre and the pull of the 'show'. That's what a successful experience looks like to me, something the audience remembers years later.

Overall, I think the main change I've seen in this industry over the years is that we're a lot more professional than we used to be. Event organisation has always required intense planning, but now it's also about the pre and post event, the accountability, the ROI, the economic impacts, audience reach, social reach and there are a lot more event organisers and planners in the marketplace, a lot more degree courses out there, and a lot of students doing professional qualifications; and there's a lot more emerging destinations to hold events in, and they're all making it easier and more interesting by building and opening up new venues and spaces.

When I started out in the industry there were no Event degrees. There was Hotel and Catering Management, there was Catering Administration, there was Hospitality Management, but there wasn't Event Management. That probably came in ten years ago and now everybody does it. But I do not think a degree is necessarily essential to succeed in this industry. I've taken on people who have absolutely no background in events or relevant degree at all, but I think they've got the right personality. Like I said before, the events industry is not for the faint-hearted. Things are going

THE EVENT PROFESSIONAL'S HANDBOOK

to go wrong and they always will, but if you're somebody who can cope with that, that's the kind of person I want. If you're somebody who can always remain cheerful in the face of screaming people, you can juggle lots of things, can think of a million things all at the same time and still keep all the balls up in the air, are not easily overcome with stress and have a sense of humour, then those abilities, to me, are much more important than experience or a qualification. I think you can tell by somebody's enthusiasm and charisma what they're going to be like. I always employ people based on that instead of their career track.

We're lucky here at London & Partners that we're a very small organisation, so I don't think we've ever actually put an advert out and gone through a specific recruitment process. But even then there are the standout people who just go the extra mile to show they're willing to not just do the task you've given them, but are the ones coming to you with suggestions of how to do things differently. They're very proactive.

I don't advocate that you have to work all the hours under the sun to impress me at all, but if you do a good job in the time that you're here then it's good enough for me. It's being enthusiastic, enjoying your job, it's thinking in an innovative and creative way, if you can save time and money on doing things. We have people that don't necessarily work here but they do volunteering. I've had a few students that have said if you need anybody to come and help, we'd love to do that. And I've just signed on to be a mentor, so having just read the CVs of many people, you can see who are different. They really want to make a difference, not just personally but in the industry and the world.

The generation that's coming through now are all about collecting experiences. They want to travel, they want to explore, which is very different to perhaps my generation, which was more about knowledge. This is something we really need to take into account moving into the future of events, to create something more immersive, more personalised. Maybe one day soon we'll all be microchipped so that when somebody is talking on the screen they'll be calling you by name or referring to you personally. I think wearable technology will become a very important part of our near future too.

Tech is obviously going to become more important. We just have to make sure it's an enabler more than a showpiece. But already you can see the benefits with helping with measurement, with personalising the experience, with identifying the right audience and improving the experience. Years ago it was the video in the machine that only worked half the time. Now it's all about virtual graphics that make you feel as though you're actually in the projected space. If you think of how far we've come in the last five to ten years, just think about what the world and this industry could be like in fifty years.

However, I do believe face-to-face will always be important. A lot of people speculate as to whether we'll all be sitting in a box at home attending meetings in the virtual world, but I don't think we will. At any event, networking is a key part of it and the more we become home-workers, the more we sit in front of screens, the more we will crave face-to-face engagement, and that's when ideas happen and collaborations happen, so live events will always be relevant.

THE
CHANGING
FACE
OF
SPONSORSHIP

CHRIS HORNBUCKLE
FOUNDER, SPORTS OPTIMUS

I t may seem strange to find a chapter on sponsorship sitting alongside more obvious topics in a book for event professionals, but there is no getting away from it, sponsorship is becoming more and more important for brands as they look to compete in an evolving marketing and communications landscape. That is not a subject for discussion in this chapter, but what is considered is the increasing importance of experiences within sponsorship activation strategy, to engage and interact with a more enlightened consumer. Those experiences are delivered digitally and of course, through events and experiential activity.

Everywhere you look, traditional models of marketing communication are in a state of flux. Traditional TV platforms, previously challenged by the introduction of satellite and Pay TV channels, are becoming even more threatened by the introduction of digital and mobile viewing platforms. Whilst everyone is familiar with YouTube and the like, new technology being presented through existing social media platforms, such as Periscope, is changing the way that digital content is created, delivered and consumed. This means that traditional sponsorship models, measured and evaluated based on media value, are becoming far less relevant, certainly for the bigger blue-chip brands. What matters now, or should matter to sponsor brands, is the connection to and the engagement with the consumer.

Other industry sectors are also experiencing significant disruption, with brands such as Uber and Airbnb challenging the traditional model. They are seeking to engage with a digital savvy audience, delivering a great service direct to the consumer. The challenge for brands and sponsors is how to embrace this changing landscape and become a disruptor rather than a disruptee!

What this means for sponsorship is clear – the old traditional model is dying. Rights holders and event owners need to reflect this in the way they package and sell their rights, ensuring that they are able to provide the rights and assets that sponsors can use productively. On the other hand, sponsor brands need to re-evaluate what they sponsor, how they activate their sponsorship and how they measure their success.

To be a truly successful sponsorship the brand needs to deliver an engagement that enhances the experience of their target audience and only then will they be accepted as part of the experience and passion that the consumer feels for their team, sport or country. Fortunately, live events and experiential activity plays a significant part in that!!

If the brand is not looking to achieve this engagement and interaction, then the sponsorship is not much more than a glorified media buy – and indeed many of the biggest sponsorships, certainly in the Barclays Premier League, are exactly that. In these cases the brands have little or no presence in the UK market and have bought expensive shirt sponsorships based on media evaluation figures, provided by the club, and particularly influenced by the overseas media values.

An example of this would be Chang Beer at Everton. Whilst they have been a partner for some time, the association and media provided by the deal in Asian markets is far more important than engaging with the club's core supporter base in the UK. Emirates is another example where the media exposure provided by a relationship with Arsenal takes precedence over any opportunity to activate around the stadium or at matches – given that their flights are full, who are we to argue with this strategy?

The changing demands of the marketplace and potential sponsors presents a significant challenge for rights holders and event owners, with many struggling to keep up with the pace of change needed to ensure they remain current. The old-style package of boards and boxes no longer works for the progressive brands, but ensuring that the rights package provides a broad enough scope of rights to allow the brand to activate creatively is hard, particularly in a digital environment where clubs, teams and players may be uncomfortable operating.

So why is this?

Firstly, because on many occasions the rights owner doesn't have and isn't providing the level of rights package needed or maybe don't understand that the things they are doing could be packaged differently and provided to the sponsor. All rights owners should be encouraged to undertake a process of "Asset Growth" – evaluating what they have and what they do from a sponsor perspective in order to grow their asset base and ultimately monetise their assets more efficiently.

And sponsors should be more forceful in pushing the rights holder to carry out this process – don't be afraid to push the rights holder, it's a buyers market after all!

Secondly, and far more of a challenge for the brands, is the rights owner wanting to retain all of the most engaging opportunities for themselves. This is particularly prevalent in the digital space where content is king. If a club only has certain levels of access to players, the digital department are reluctant to allow the partners "first dibs" on that access, preferring to retain the juiciest opportunities for themselves.

Both of these are completely contrary to the principles of providing the consumer with an ever-improved user experience – building an engaged community is surely the main aim of club and brand, irrespective of who gets the credit for that, and in actual fact, the club has probably sold that opportunity to the brand who just gets frustrated at the lack of support. Numerous examples from my own past have seen requests to film content with the club captain or star player be rejected for unspecified reasons, only to see that player feature in club-generated content a week later.

Getting back to events then, and taking a broader definition to include experiential marketing activity and how this is being impacted by the changing sponsorship landscape.

If you agree with the premise that to be a successful sponsorship then you need to look "beyond the boards" and really understand consumer engagement, then two key pillars of any effective sponsorship activation have to be a strong digital and content strategy, and an engaging experiential platform with the premise of enhancing the consumer experience. Linking the two pillars is the fact that events provide the perfect backdrop for creating great digital content – giving the fans at home the opportunity to experience the atmosphere at the game, for example.

On that basis, this is a great opportunity for the event and experiential industry to make inroads into the sponsorship activation strategies of brands. But what events should you be looking to create, and how do you deliver value?

Taking the first of those questions, what events work in a sponsorship content?

To answer that I'll use an example from my own working experience. At Vauxhall, as sponsors of the England football team, we were looking to create a stronger engagement with the consumers who were supporting the national team during the UEFA European Championships 2012 in Poland and Ukraine. In actual fact, we were looking to position ourselves as a supporter of England, and a friend to the fans, giving them something to enhance their experience of the match and tournament. Hopefully, this would start to change their perception of Vauxhall as a brand and ultimately drive consideration for the product.

Whatever we created would become a critical part of the campaign and would supplement our TV advert, media exposure through a talkSPORT relationship and other digital and in-store activity.

We ran a number of Fan Hubs in all the venue cities in Ukraine where England played, plus a number at home in the UK. We provided access to fans who were part of the official travelling party, and assorted winners of various competitions run through the media partner and our own digital platforms. Inside the Fan Hubs we provided entertainment, expert analysis from football legends, competitions and prizes, and perhaps most importantly for many of the supporters, a safe place where they could come together with other England fans ahead of the game.

What resulted was fantastic – several thousand England fans taking over a square in Donetsk, hanging their flags out and turning the area into a mini-Wembley. Unquestionably the fan experience was enhanced that day.

This was extended back to the UK, with digital content created in and around the Fan Hub, extending the reach of the activity, making it more cost-effective in terms of fans reached, and delivering a feeling of being in Ukraine for the tournament. The overriding view of the supporters was that the whole event enhanced their match day experience and provided something that they don't normally get.

Interestingly, whilst the Fan Hubs were done in conjunction with England, indeed ticket collections and Supporters Club liaison was done from the venues, the activity used very few of the actual sponsorship rights (given that these are significantly restricted during tournament time anyway).

In my view, this was a perfect example of an event or experiential activation that enhanced the match day experience for the consumer, not just "live" in the venue, but extended back across multiple venues and beyond through digital content into the consumers' living rooms.

However, you don't necessarily need to go to these lengths to run a successful sponsorship event – anything that rewards supporters or helps them to enjoy their day can work equally well. An often quoted example of this is O2 and the great work they do through their Rewards programme. I like the O2 Pavilion at Twickenham, and have often stood in the cold and wet of the West Car Park looking up from my Vodafone phone to the O2 tent. What a great way to reward loyal O2 customers than to give them somewhere warm and dry to drink prior to an England match – restricting access to those with an O2 phone is certainly a great thank you to their customers.

In fact, anything that adds value to the consumer's day is a worthy event and should be encouraged by the rights holder – we all want the consumer to enjoy the experience, as that's what drives return visits, further purchases and brand affiliation. Brands are usually far better placed to deliver this, and if you can convince them that the value return is justifiable as part of the activation budget, then you're in with a chance!

In terms of how to add value, working closely with the rights owner certainly helps, and if you can identify some shared goals for the activity then they will certainly get behind it. At Liverpool, Vauxhall worked closely with the club to help develop the Family Zone, adding games and competitions into an existing and successful area. The result was an even more exciting and interesting experiential solution that benefited club, brand and most importantly the supporters.

So, this has to be the right time for event organisers and experiential organisations to "dip their toe" into the sponsorship waters. Rights holders and brands should be looking to increase consumer engagement, and generally need help, probably from event professionals, to understand how to do that.

Look at Manchester City and their match day ambassadors – a simple concept to help supporters of both the home and away teams get more out of their visit to the stadium and attendance at the game. A truly innovative activation by the club, delivered by an event and experiential agency. But why couldn't that have been a sponsor initiative? What an amazing activation it would have been and a simple way of engaging with supporters, providing some added value and instantly becoming part of the match day experience. If that isn't going to enhance brand perception then I don't know what will!

The challenge will ultimately come in convincing the brands that events in this sponsorship space can add value to the sponsorship activation, but it can't always be about logo placement anymore. Consumers want more and events can be the way to provide that!

BUMS ON SEATS:

OF

AUDIENCE ACQUISITION

SIMON HUGHES
MANAGING PARTNER,
MCHA LTD

Context: Simon Hughes has worked in creative industry roles for over 30 years and currently runs a consultancy providing strategic and tactical services to the event sector. He spent ten years working in the Central Office of Information (COI), the UK government marketing communications agency which devised and delivered government communication campaigns.

In his role as Director of Live Events he worked on many complex event projects, such as the one described below involving the UK Cabinet. This is composed of the Prime Minister and the most senior government ministers and is the collective decision-making body of Her Majesty's Government that traditionally meets every week. The work of the Cabinet is supported by the Cabinet Office who work very closely with the Prime Minister's staff that operate out of Number 10 Downing Street.

f you search for the phrase "bums on seats" you'll see that it has been appropriated by both politicians and the airline business, even though it was apparently coined back in the 80s to describe the paying audience at a venue. It is in many ways a rather derogatory term but nonetheless remains one of the most important elements for many events regardless of type – from conferences to festivals, exhibitions to congresses. As the author James Grant put it, "It's about bums on seats. If nobody wants to listen to what you are doing, it kind of defeats the purpose really, doesn't it?"

Among the many events I was asked to produce during my time as Director of Live Events for the COI, the UK government marketing communications agency, the constant challenge was finding the right people to attend them – getting enough bums on seats to ensure success. Within the insular world of the UK Civil Service, policy teams often thought that the new policy or legislation they were grappling with was the most important thing in the whole world. My team knew otherwise and there were constant struggles to reach out to the right people to fill the events that we were commissioned to produce in support of key government communication campaigns.

I clearly remember the look of absolute horror on the faces of the team behind GM Nation – the national debate on genetically modified food and technology – when I suggested that the issue of GM was probably not even in the top 100 list of things that ordinary people were worrying about right then. Given that they were all experts on either side of the debate and passionately engaged in the subject, my suggestion that David Beckham's latest hairstyle was of more interest was possibly not the most diplomatic thing to say, even though it was probably true.

So what did this constant struggle to get bums on seats teach me? Firstly, that you have to have a really flexible and creative team around you that are prepared to put the hard slog in to make things happen. There is no way of sugar-coating this – it's hard work that requires relentless follow up and dedication. You have to be prepared to jump over hurdles constantly, always smile when you dial when you (inevitably) have to hit the phones, and celebrate every success to keep you motivated. Even the knock backs that you encounter on a regular basis as you chase the all-important numbers down can be used to focus effort and improve your efficiency.

Having a flexible resource means working with people that bring a number of complementary skills together. This can include people with a background in research who know where to source information and how to access both networks and lists to add to the initial target audience database. It means having people that can collate and analyse data effectively and can produce spreadsheets in their sleep. Above all, it means having people who are really good with people and can communicate efficiently and effectively no matter who they are contacting.

I also quite deliberately have used the word creative because you will need to be creative in your approach to getting those bums on seats. Like any selling job it's not just about what you are saying – listening carefully to the responses you get can create more opportunities and new contacts. Creativity is also required in crafting the right messaging for different types of potential audience members as well as the different channels you'll be using to reach them. Creativity allows you the freedom to make mistakes that can then inform better performance, so be prepared to take risks and test ideas out.

One project that certainly required plenty of creativity in our approach to audience acquisition were the series of regional Cabinet meetings that took us around the UK visiting cities such as Birmingham, Glasgow, Liverpool, Exeter, Southampton, Cardiff, Leeds and Durham. Each meeting involved a public session, where an invited audience met with all the Cabinet members and was then followed by a formal Cabinet meeting. As you can imagine the rather intense security required played a huge part in the planning process, not least in the way that we invited and then vetted our audiences. Our starting point was a look at the National Census data for each city/region. This gave us the basic demographic information that would drive our audience segmentation, with the aim being that the final selection of people that we assembled should be a reasonably representative selection of the local population.

Our audience brief was put rather more succinctly by one of the No.10 staffers: "We don't want a room full of middle-aged white people thinking they are the great and the good." Having established some fairly fixed targets in terms of gender, age and ethnic origin we then factored in statistics around employment and employers to ensure that all the major businesses in the region were on our radar. The key aim was to avoid ending up with the usual suspects – which meant that we then had to go through lists provide by local MPs, the local Government Office, the Regional Development Agency etc. and cherry-pick those that fitted the profiles we'd developed for the event.

This could of course have become a rather haphazard process and involved a lot of diplomatic manoeuvring and liaison with our client team at the Cabinet Office – so establishing clear reporting protocols and schedules so that we could update them on daily progress was an essential way of managing both the process and their expectations. It also helped to ensure that those awkward conversations that occasionally arose when a local bigwig spat the dummy at not being invited were managed as effectively as possible. Promises of bottles of whiskey from the House of Commons were of course never used – certainly not in writing.

As with any event one of the priorities was ensuring that the client team felt confident about not only our overall approach but also that progress was being made – often against quite challenging timeframes. Account management of this kind demands that you not only produce the data required in a timely manner but that you also anticipate questions and challenges, particularly if progress is slow. Like many clients the demands being made on them to deliver were extreme and it was critical that we created a real sense of trust and confidence in our ability to deliver all aspects of the event to time and budget.

This brings me to a particularly peculiar aspect of this project in terms of how content in event marketing has to be handled. Given the extraordinary security arrangements that needed to be put in place we had to develop a two-stage audience acquisition process. For obvious reasons we could not actually tell the people that we were inviting much about what we were inviting them to. Our initial task therefore was to contact the right mix of people and establish if they were available on a specific date to attend a "major national Government event". No more details were allowed to be given and they were then invited to register their interest on a website. Without giving away any of the dark arts involved, this first step allowed a vetting process to be undertaken.

If they cleared that hurdle we would confirm that a personal invite would be issued shortly before the event. The security protocols meant that there was always a complete news blackout until 24 hours before the event took place, by which time the security operation around the designated venue had been established and detailed invites were then sent to the approved audience members. By the time they arrived, local media had usually been briefed so they knew roughly what to expect – but we'd had to get them to commit with very little information on the actual nature or indeed content of the event.

Our official status as a government agency was obviously a huge plus in this regard, as was the tremendous support of the extended teams in the Local Government Offices that we worked with. One way of off-setting the limited spaces available at the public meeting was to organise a series of regional visits for the Cabinet members to attend either before or after the main meeting – so they would turn up at major employers, universities and hospitals as part of their away day from Westminster. This meant that we could factor into our audience acquisition the other planned activities and visits and avoid targeting people that would be otherwise engaged in part of the overall activity.

Still, it was a rather odd way of having to deal with getting the right number (and type) of bums of seats and certainly taught me some important lessons about the value of content marketing to drive demand. First, your event content should be framed in a holistic manner, so that the people that will be attending become as important as the actual content they will share. This certainly worked for the historic series of regional Cabinet meetings. If we needed some local charity groups to be represented then telling one that several others had already signed up frequently moved their level of engagement forward; the same approach applied across many other sectors as well. The use of peer pressure and brand association to drive interest and engagement to the point where people actually commit their valuable time to attend your event should not be underestimated.

The second key thing about content marketing that strikes me as I reflect on this rather extraordinary set of events is the power of storytelling. My brilliant team could not actually tell anyone the real story but could create a clear sense of something genuinely unique, shrouded in mystery (yet all the more compelling because of that) and uniquely personalised. We wanted the people we contacted to understand that they had been chosen specifically because we wanted them to have the opportunity to share and learn more face-to-face in a gathering that would benefit them and the organisation they represented or worked for.

So if we extrapolate that kind of approach into the real world, then telling the story of the event to the target audience isn't a bad way to approach the development of any event marketing plan. It means that your storylines can involve the other people that are attending as well as the actual content. It allows creative freedom to tell the story of the overall experience that they will share – not just the content itself. The variety of formats being deployed, the types of activities that they could select from, the opportunity for them to build a personal itinerary within the event – all of these form storylines to engage your potential audience with.

Whilst content is king in many ways – just look at the use of headline acts in many music festivals – getting the big marquee names confirmed on your agenda is just part of the story you should be telling. The ubiquitous use of social media creates many more opportunities to get conversations going that are linked to what the big name brands are going to be saying as well as what your potential audience wants to hear more about. Engaging with your content providers in order to identify key storylines and then use them to drive audience engagement is obviously a critical part of developing a compelling story.

My final thought is around the end of the experience – when you've got all the right bums on all the seats available and the whole thing has gone to plan. One of the key features about the regional Cabinet meetings was the impact on the invited audience of being so directly engaged by senior members of the UK Government – each table was hosted by a Cabinet member during the public meeting session. In that sense we stuck to the story we'd used to get them along in the first place – this really was a unique opportunity and they did have the chance to ask hard questions and get real responses firsthand. An unexpected bonus was that the then Prime Minister Gordon Brown really came into his own when talking to them all – many expressed their surprise at his passion, engagement and conviction – a very different performance in a live setting when compared to his usual media persona.

Capture that feedback. Make sure you get quotes, clips and evidence of how much people enjoyed the overall experience. You will have a story to tell for another time and real feedback will help you tell it more convincingly. Your clients will also value it and it will add value to the next time you set off to get more bums on seats. Good luck.

THE
ATTENDEE
EXPERIENCE
OF THE
FUTURE
– WILL YOU BE READY?

BRIAN LUDWIG
SENIOR VICE PRESIDENT,
CVENT

Technology is all around us. We use it in every aspect of our lives, and in many cases we have grown to take its presence and the impact it has on our existence for granted. As new technologies evolve, they provide us with the opportunities to do even more amazing things and when put into the context of events, they open up a world of opportunity for both organisers and attendees.

Technology is evolving at an exponential rate whilst simultaneously becoming more accessible to the everyday user. In order to remain at the top of their game in an arena, which is notoriously competitive, meetings and event organisers need to constantly be evaluating, innovating and improving their offerings.

To put this into perspective, over 100 years ago it took 26 years for a quarter of the US population to own a television. In the late 90s it took half that time (13 years) for quarter of that population to start using mobile phones. Bring that forward to today, and recent statistics show that is has taken a mere three years for quarter of the US population to own and use a tablet (Pew Research Center/Economist).

The rate at which this technology has become more accessible and commonplace in our lives has also had significant changes on our behaviour as consumers, both in terms of the way we communicate with others and with regard to the speed at which we have grown to expect things to happen for us.

We now live in a society where we become agitated at the fact the wi-fi has 'gone down' during an international flight, with many of us no longer stopping to think about the fact that we are flying at approximately 550mph at a sustained altitude of 36,000ft is a miracle in itself – instead we grimace that our smartphone is failing to load our latest news feed.

The Internet and social media have not only changed the way we communicate, but it has transformed our everyday wants and needs. We have become reliant on having everything instantly at our fingertips. Recent analysis has shown in each minute of 2016, there are 20.8m WhatsApp messages sent, 150m emails sent and 2.4m Google search queries (Excelacom, Inc 2016).

Events create a unique space where event organisers are beginning to fuse digital technologies with the real world and in doing so, are able to sculpt attendee experiences and we believe we are now seeing just the early stages of how technology and innovation will ultimately impact meetings and events. In order to continue down this path, organisers will need to readily embrace new-age technologies and harness their enormous power to deliver seamless and engaging attendee experiences of the future and perhaps that future is not too distant.

THE EVENT PROFESSIONAL'S HANDBOOK

ATTENDEE EXPERIENCE – TRAVELLING TO AN EVENT

Airports are getting smarter with more prevalent automated check-in services and new electronic passports that can speed up the formalities of travelling whilst reducing the need for airport personnel. Soon we will see people breeze through their gate and board the plane not only without showing a paper ticket but without scanning a QR code on their mobile either.

Virgin Atlantic utilises Apple's iBeacon technology at airports such as London Heathrow. Upper Class passengers (with Apple Passbook downloaded) approaching security can now automatically be sent a notification, directly to their phone, prompting them to open their electronic boarding pass ready for scanning ahead of their arrival at security. We are also increasingly seeing the use of iBeacons as a marketing tool in the main halls of the airports, feeding passengers using the service with special discounted partner offers, such as 0% commission as they pass a particular currency exchange booth.

TRANSFERS AND ACCOMMODATION

Recent research conducted by Exelacom has confirmed that this year (2016), 1389 Uber transfers are being requested per minute. That's a lot of transfers being requested on demand and as the populations' access to smartphones increase, so too will need for transport 'on demand'.

Driverless cars is a notion politicians across London have recently taken an interest in, as a means to address the housing crisis which is one of the biggest challenges facing England's capital today. Building more homes for London's growing population requires space and cars do tend to take up a lot of space! Self-driven cars take up much less space, they are safer, smaller and don't have to be there when you don't need them.

This concept may seem farfetched in terms of practical implementation for the here and now, but it's only a matter of time until we see this technology materialise. These ambitious proposals supported in the May 2016 Queen's Speech not only ensure that the UK will remain at the forefront of technology, but they also hold a great deal of opportunity when applied to the means in which we transport our delegates to and from events.

That's not all when it comes to travel; mobile hotel check-in is already being adopted by the likes of Starwood Hotels, who are upgrading their offering to provide a seamless check-in experience. Guests can now pre-select a room from their device and then use keyless entry to gain access directly from their smartphones.

ATTENDEE EXPERIENCE ONSITE
SELF-SERVE REGISTRATION AT EVENTS

Registration is one of the first major touch points that delegates have with your event, so it's vital the process is both seamless and impressive. One of our most popular products at Cvent is our self-serve registration software, allowing attendees to check-in themselves and print their own badge.

Any tablet or smartphone connected to the Internet can function as a self-service, onsite kiosk, allowing guests to register, check-in, pay, check-in their guests, and preview/edit/print their name badge all on their own.

WEARABLE TECHNOLOGY AND AUGMENTED REALITY

We've already witnessed a huge leap forward in the use of wearable technology and ever since Google launched its Google Glass project, the reality of wearable eyewear seems to be inevitable. Since then, developers have desperately been trying to match the Google Glass offering, by creating their own wearable display glasses. What started out as a futuristic phenomenon used by only a few, is now finally making its way from the mainstream world into events and exhibitions and this exciting technology holds so much potential when considering its application.

One of the key advantages wearable technology and augmented reality can bring to an event is by providing a more tailored and personal experience for all of its attendees. The technology can also vastly enhance productivity by facilitating networking among guests and tailoring streams of information. The enabling of location services using augmented reality can also help guests find their way around the venue – with markers placed on floor plans and maps that bring up event schedules and information on demand. Imagine a day when an attendee sees contextual info hovering above exhibitors, above attendees, above sponsors, etc. Time is valuable at an event and technology will enable everyone to get the most out of that precious time.

PROXIMITY COMMUNICATIONS MARKETING AND GEOFENCING

Communication is an activity with an intrinsic social effect; the more people we can communicate with on any given platform, the greater the value of that platform to us. Imagine a world where your attendees are sent customised messages to their mobile device as they walk into a certain area on the show floor? It's called 'proximity marketing', and it's set to make a major splash in the world of events.

Ever since beacon technology came about, beacons have been touted as bringing about a revolution for proximity-based communication. Exhibitions and events lend themselves so well to this technology as their implementation can create a much more productive environment for attendees, guiding them through a personalised experience which is tailored to each of their attendance objectives.

Geofencing is another example of this technology, defining a virtual boundary around a real-world geographical area, an event venue. In doing so, event organisers can create a radius of interest and this can be used to trigger an action such as a message, promotion or an alert to a smart device.

NAVIGATION ASSISTANCE

Navigation assistance is another technology which is going to have a notable impact on events and large-scale conferences in the long term. Event mobile apps lay out detailed floor plans. Beacons or RFID now allow for indoor geolocation awareness. The two together can allow an organiser to serve up a "door-to-door" path from where the attendee is standing to where he or she would like to be next. Layer in some augmented reality on top of this scenario as the true "cherry on top", in which attendees can literally see the optimal path through the event labyrinth which will foster more networking, more collaboration, and more consumption of amazing content – and in the end, that's what events are all about.

REMOTE PRESENCE

Many of you will be familiar with technologies such as Apple Facetime or Skype which allow you to talk in real time to friends, family and colleagues. As this software becomes the norm, we are only just scratching the surface when considering how further advancements in remote presence will impact both events and, in a more general context, business models.

Remote presence technologies provide both a practical and cost-effective alternative to face-to-face meetings by providing virtual business representatives, stand personnel or product experts who can interface with attendees live via an iPad. The iPad mounted onto something like a Segway, which is being controlled remotely, really brings the interaction to a different level. And we see a future in which robotics will play a role in this paradigm shift as well.

CONTENT AND ENGAGEMENT
NEW PERSPECTIVES

Mark Zuckerberg, Chairman, Chief Executive and Co-founder of Facebook, commented recently in a seminar on the interesting transition we are seeing with regards to traditional video content blending with more immersive content. Zuckerberg states that when you think about virtual reality, a lot of people first think about gaming but he believes video will be more engaging in a lot of ways.

360 or spherical videos began to go mainstream around June 2015 and it looks like the technology is set for greater growth in 2016. The videos, which can be shot in all directions, typically with multiple cameras, create immersive experiences for viewers. When applied to the world of events, this technology has the potential to revolutionise the way we deliver educational seminars and other digital content.

Secondary to this, drones are now popping up in some really interesting places, including events! Their versatility is allowing event organisers to capture imagery which has never before been caught. Sweeping views of speeches over an enraptured audience or a unique venue layout from a new high vantage point can serve as a way to keep attendees excited about the event they are part of, or a way to keep remote attendees engaged, or as incredible marketing materials to draw attendees to the next event.

HOLOGRAMS

The use of 3D holographic technology has the potential to transform an event through either amplifying an experience, creating something unforgettable, or equally, on a practical level by creating a holographic image in the form of a person or object which has the capabilities of reaching a global audience without the cost of travel.

This technology will provide global organisations with a vehicle to connect and engage with their audience in a single live event. Holograms are a major technological development in the world of events as they have the potential to provide us with new ways to visualise our work as well as new ways to share conceptual ideas with each other.

Taking this one step further, researchers from the Digital Nature Group (DNG) at Japan's University of Tsukuba, have now reported that they have come up with a way to render touchable, aerial images in real-time using lasers, mirrors, lenses, and clever programming which when eventually applied to the world of events, will enhance attendee engagement on a whole new level.

CROWDSOURCED AND REAL-TIME CONTENT

Interactive presentation apps such as Glisser or live video sharing via Snapchat or Periscope are becoming much more popular in the event space, as they have the capabilities of instantly capturing speaker and presentation content and broadcasting it to the wider world in real time.

In the five years since its launch, Snapchat has evolved enormously and according to a report by CNBC, it was the most used app at the South by Southwest® Conference & Festival – with thousands of users downloading it for the first time in Austin. The app now receives more than 8 billion video views every day and has 100 million daily active users.

The rapid evolution of Snapchat has had a profound effect on the live event industry with the 'Stories', curated by the app, broadcasting content in real time from a specific location or event for 24 hours at a time, which create real and immediate value for those involved.

When applied correctly, this technology will also provide conference organisers with more awareness regarding their delegates and what makes them tick. Exhibitions and events which use these apps effectively, will be able to make the most of the advancements in technology and the extra layer of intelligence they offer to both the event organiser and attendee.

CONCLUSION

If we step back and take a view on the evolution of technology within the events space over the past few years, it is clear to see it is beginning to play an integral role. And we expect this trend to only accelerate over the next five to ten years, touching every phase of the event experience including before, during and after. Some technologies are here today and will simply become far more pervasive in the events industry as time marches on. Others are yet to make their way to any event organisers just yet – but they will. In the words of Sir Richard Branson, 'Every success story is a tale of constant adaption, revision and change.' I foresee organisers putting these words into practice by leveraging the latest and greatest technology to transform events into experiences.

PRODUCING

BRILLIANT

EXPERIENCES

— IS A —

BALANCE BETWEEN
ART AND SCIENCE

JASON MEGSON
MANAGING DIRECTOR,
GEORGE P. JOHNSON

I t was 18 years ago when I first started in the events industry, as a hardworking rigger in the very early days of crewing company Gallowglass. I think one of the unique aspects of my career journey has been the opportunity to work my way around a number of different areas in the events business which has always opened-up new and exciting opportunities. After Gallowglass, I started working with some of the marketing communications agencies who were my clients at the time. They initially asked me to come on board as a project manager leading a large retailer's account. So that piqued my interest in terms of what, in those very early days, experiential marketing was.

After a rather enjoyable stint working at an advertising agency in Australia for a year, I decided to take a degree in Economics and Politics as a mature student at Edinburgh University and then made the big move to London with the perhaps crazy idea of becoming a stockbroker. But I always kept my foot in the industry door, and thankfully, after the market crash dashed my stockbroking ambitions, I had some fantastic previous experience to fall back on. So for the past eight years I've been in London, I've been lucky enough to work for some of the best integrated and specialist experience marketing agencies including Ogilvy, BD Network and Because, plus I even found the time to start my own agency, WeFew. All of which has helped land my current role, Managing Director of the world's premier experiential marketing agency, George P. Johnson (GPJ). Quite a journey, but I don't regret any part of it.

Truthfully, at the very start of my career, I don't think I was perhaps as committed to it as I could have been. A few people have similar stories where back then, they just sort of fell into "doing events". We didn't go to the careers advisor and say "I want to work in experience marketing". I think I actually told them I wanted to be a car designer, or maybe even something clichéd like an astronaut. I suppose that I might have moved a little quicker in terms of career progression had I embraced it sooner, but then I'm a big believer in looking forward without looking back. I'm really pleased at where I've managed to get to in this industry, but some of that has been more by luck than design.

I love the fact that producing brilliant experiences is a beautiful balance between art and science. You have the science part that involves being highly organised and committed to delivery, fused with the art of producing big ideas that have the power to change the way people feel and create meaningful memories. Engagement is one of those terms which is bandied about a lot. For me it all starts with understanding what engages the audience first. If you focus on the individual, then engagement should at least create some sense of excitement and emotional reaction in them. On the back of that, the emotional reactions should pertain to a sense of optimism, that something is going to happen next and there are future possibilities that didn't exist prior to the engagement.

One of the most enjoyable parts of this job is finding new talent. I think it comes back to my previous point about art and science – you want to see someone with ambition and drive which is hugely important, because if you are to be successful in this industry you can't just plod along. It moves very fast and it's changed a lot in a short space of time. So you have to be ambitious and willing to take on opportunities. But with that ambition, you need to have a bit of entrepreneurial flair and you need to be able to take risks, albeit couched within the realms of what's physically possible and what isn't. And I think that's the nice balance. The majority of people that I know in this industry start from having the basic skills or "the craft" as I sometimes call it – they understand what it takes to put on a successful event – but then the ones that really stand out are those who know how to push the boundaries and strive to create something new. The ideas that are really memorable and become hugely successful experiences are created and managed by those who take risks and have that creative spark in their DNA.

I don't think an events specific degree is essential, but I do think it's a very good starting point. There's a sense of discipline and some fundamental learning that students who do event management courses will pick up, and in some ways they might be slightly ahead of other people who want to come into the industry who haven't gone to university. But I'm all for people coming from different backgrounds. So I think in certain areas if you want to be a bit more of a specialist then a period of study can help and accelerate your career. But for the team at GPJ, it's not a base level requirement that you must have. I think if we were to become an agency that made a degree mandatory then we'd be a little bit homogenised and lacking in creativity. Because a lot of the university courses are focused on not taking risks – the course structure is about those (albeit important) matters like health and safety, production planning and seeking the right permissions.

When GPJ takes people on board, we have a mentorship program that's quite informal. We tend to identify those who we think are going to be the future stars and high performers, and those are the people we attach the first senior mentors to, to make sure we can support them in realising their potential. And I'm all for pushing people into positions where they might feel like they're out of their depth, because that tends to be when the real talent flourishes. It's also fair to say that others may go on a slightly different trajectory. They may be more of the slow and steady types, but they still have a long and fruitful future with the agency. So we just pick little points along the journey of their career where we can light a little fire under them and get them moving faster, or perhaps give them additional training and support along the way.

Nurturing talent is also about giving individuals a chance to celebrate their successes, but importantly to celebrate those successes as a team. Because it's a hugely collaborative and team-focused business, you just can't be successful if you can't work well in a team. Highlighting team successes, especially with some of the newer or perhaps more junior team members, is important, as we're only as strong as our weakest link. I also think it's important to celebrate failures too. Have a rant, swear a bit, go for a drink, relax. It's important because then you can draw a line under it and move on. We occasionally work long and unsociable hours, so the time we spend celebrating or commiserating after a tough project or pitch is key.

One of the challenges we face is that we're losing some very talented people that could be fantastic within our industry to other places that seem more immediately compelling. For example, we could be losing them to technology start-ups that are perhaps more progressive in how they think about their business, their products and the impact they have on society. The graduate and school-leaving generation of today are going to be more attracted to this in some cases, and hence we have to up our game in order to both attract and retain talent.

I think the future of this industry is only going to become more competitive, as many more agencies that don't come from a legacy of event management and production will be entering our space. They see the value that brand experience has in terms of consumers. So there'll be media agencies, digital agencies, ad agencies, all encroaching on our nice little world. It's already happening. In some ways this is nothing to be worried about and it's healthy, plus it means that we'll be able to attract talent from places where we wouldn't normally look. At GPJ we've already been hiring great people from advertising and digital agencies, so that kind of competition is exciting. But I think it will be tough and only the strongest agencies with the most savvy and committed clients will get the best out of experience marketing in the next five to ten years.

I think how we as an industry respond to and work with technology in the future is a fascinating matter. Already we have experiences that are anti-technology. They bar participants from using their phones or even sharing their experience online. And increasing amounts of people are paying the premium to be in that space where they are deprived of the technology they spend 90% of their lives focused on and are almost reconnecting with traditional ways of communicating and socialising.

If you were a teenager in the 1970s, you didn't have any way of communicating with your friends digitally or barely even on the phone, so you spent your time hanging out with them in the local neighbourhood. You probably did that 80% of the time, and now that's completely flipped. We would probably pay money to hang out and play football in the street with our mates now. It's become a novelty. We're getting to the point where real-world experiences will become more valuable and more intense, almost concentrated, because people will pay for authenticity and the face-to-face human interaction they provide.

One of the interesting things technology does is that it helps us to collect lots more data about people's behaviours and their habits, and it also gives us the chance to react nearly in real time to people's wants and needs. And so one of the big questions in the future of experiences will likely revolve around permission. Technology will give us opportunities to do exciting things with people as long as they give us permission to do them.

Just like when you think of the rise of immersive theatre productions like Punchdrunk, you know you're going into an experience where you'll potentially be out of your comfort zone. I think we'll be able to produce those kinds of experiences for brands and people in the real world, but I think there will be an interesting tipping point when people stop giving permission for certain things. But that does mean there will be other opportunities to be even more out-there and more creative when people say "I'm all yours, you can do whatever you want. You can hook me up with wearables, you can access my social media accounts, you can change the experience in real time depending on the temperature of my palms or how red my lips are…" All these things will be possible, but the interesting thing will be how people change their behaviour and their openness to that type of experience. With so many opportunities to deliver experiences in new ways I can't think of a better and more dynamic industry to work in.

SPORTS EVENTS

NIGEL RUSHMAN
FOUNDER, RUSHMANS

David Rose certainly hit the mark when he said that businesses designed to succeed in the 20th century are doomed for failure in the 21st.

So why is it that so much of the sports events business seems to have willingly lodged itself into a time warp at around the time of the Sydney Olympic Games which straddled the two centuries; designed in the final years of the 1900s and delivered to great acclaim in the first year of the new millennium?

That was 16 years ago and I am concerned that not only has the sports event sector not really moved on but that it has become so deeply entrenched in the principles and practices that made Sydney 2000 a success that it has found a comfort zone from which it has no real desire to emerge to face the new realities of delivering events in an environment where they face new economic challenges and new levels of scrutiny from media and other stakeholders.

We must never forget that the entire sports business is built on great events. They are the core product of a global industry estimated to be worth up to $1 trillion in rights fees, sponsorship, tickets and sundry other income streams. But each of these is dependent on there being an event to sell in the first place. Major events such as the Olympic Games and the FIFA World Cup are the biggest shows on earth. It's become something of a cliché to talk about them as pure unscripted drama but it's a cliché because it's true and the massive global TV audiences they attract underscore their appeal and tremendous commercial value. For now.

But while so much about the sports business has moved over the last decade and a half, the planning and management of the events which are the foundations of this massive global business seems to have simply stood still.

The success of Sydney 2000 had a profound impact on the events sector, which has, in a number of ways, become the victim of that success. Firstly, it quickly began to be seen as a blueprint for all other events, irrespective of their scale or actual complexity. Secondly, it created a small army of workers who had been employed at Sydney whose experience – often creatively inflated on subsequent CVs – was seen as a passport to the next job where they simply replicated the processes they had learned in Australia, without thought for how they might be adapted and improved for the specific conditions and challenges of the new event.

The result is that in too many instances the evolution of the sports events sector has simply ground to a halt and that the default starting point and frame of reference for organising any event is the Olympic Games. This has created a tidal wave of waste and profligacy which could engulf sports in the decades to come.

The Rugby World Cup, staged in England in autumn 2015, was set to break all revenue records for World Rugby, the international governing body which relies on the tournament for 90% of its total income which is, in great part, ploughed back into developing the game.

This is a long tournament but one which is essentially straightforward in management terms. There is little fresh construction involved and each of the stadiums being used host big games with big crowds throughout the rugby and football seasons. Their own infrastructures, procedures and staffing are clearly up to scratch. The media and commercial aspects of Rugby World Cup are handled by the world's biggest sports marketing company, IMG, and the host broadcast role lies with another experienced and established operator, ITV Sport.

So why are so many people being employed to run Rugby World Cup? What do they all they do all day?

A number of the key individuals responsible for Rugby World Cup moved from the London 2012 Olympic Games Organising Committee which was, of course, hugely influenced by its predecessor in Sydney. London 2012 was presented as an organisational success so the systems and processes have been largely unquestioned and have, in some considerable part, been applied to Rugby World Cup.

This is, of course, a complete nonsense as there is simply no comparison between the relative levels of complexity of these events. What links them is a culture of employing way too many people on a just-in-case basis and then throwing money at problems which emerge from the cracks in thinking and planning.

In the case of many major international events the money which is being chucked around comes from the state, or more specifically from the pockets of taxpayers, but because the delivery of the event is seen as a matter of national – or at least municipal – prestige, the sort of scrutiny, checks and balances which would apply in the world of real business are simply non-existent.

In my experience there is profligacy on a grand scale and no incentive to eliminate it by embracing a style of thinking and working which applies elsewhere. The fact that a cheque can be written by government to paper over cracks in planning and management means that there is little or no incentive to change the way things are done and that, as all entrepreneurs know, is the beginning of a slippery slope.

Too many sports events exist in a cocoon, protected from the realities of external conditions. Because of the structure of sport and the inevitable links to government, too many people have too much to lose if an event is seen to fail from a financial perspective. So not only do organisers routinely overspend public money but they then commission pre- and post-event evaluations to justify them through often spurious analysis of a range of economic data.

When I consider major sports event management today I am amazed at how immature it is. But now is the time for it to grow up and grow up fast.

So much has changed in the world of business since the turn of the century but, by and large, major sports events seem to be turning a blind eye. You can understand why when embracing change would involve coming out of a comfortable warm bath and suffering the shock of the cold shower of reality. It would involve asking difficult questions about staffing, responsibility and accountability. It would, in particular, mean more stringent processes and procedures to ensure that money, whether from the private sector or taxpayers, was not being wasted in a disgraceful fashion.

Sports events right now have become so unwieldy that they have started to create their own internal demand cycles. In the simplest terms, when you employ a lot of people you create the need for an HR/personnel department which itself needs to be administered and managed. Every additional process grafted onto an organisational plan also needs to be administered and managed…and then the managers have to be managed and so on. Event people are usually 'Event People' rather than large organisational veterans, they do not have the experience of large-scale corporate management and collaboration to succeed. The result is a level of unnecessary complexity, heading off the scale fast.

Now it's not that I am advocating change in sports event management for its own sake, even though as a businessman it grieves me to think of the unnecessary waste which seem to be the inevitable by-product of current thinking and practices.

The reality is that change will ultimately be driven from within sport. In recent times we have seen a number of potential host cities and nations either pull out of, or simply not enter, the bidding process because of the cost involved. On a number of occasions this has been because citizens have voted against bidding because they are unable to see a clear and tangible link between costs and benefits. On others it has been because politicians are not willing to risk their personal capital and ultimately, careers and future influence, on schemes which will be expensive and unpopular with voters.

The fact is that potential hosts are getting smarter about the way they evaluate events and less inclined to write what appear to be open cheques drawn on the public account. The last major example of this was Oslo's decision to pull out of the 2022 Olympic Games bidding because of the cost and the burden of conditions imposed by the International Olympic Committee. This is not a trend confined to mega events, it is being seen all the way down the line.

While those cities and nations where money is not an issue and where public consultation is unheard of may continue to throw money into the machine to create events designed to show them in the best light on the international stage, it is in the long-term interests of the ultimate rights owners to achieve a balanced spread of hosts. To do that they are going to have to bring down costs.

Bringing the sports event industry into the 21st century is one way of doing that. That means interrogating every established process, using new ways of approaching and thinking-through planning, embracing appropriate new technologies and generally challenging the old ways. Right now the systems are built for maximum distraction and minimal effectiveness. That needs to be reversed.

In my 30 years of experience in this field it has become clear that the majority of the inefficiency overspend on managing events arises as a direct result of poor early strategy and planning. This leads to unnecessary complexity and money spent further down the line.

A method we use to get it right is the introduction of Structured Visual Thinking™ and the use of proven and robust collaborative processes which identify opportunities and challenges and the strategies to overcome them, and plot a clear path to successful outcomes by maximising the use of appropriate resources enabling spending to be appropriate for the desired outcome.

Along with my colleagues, we have used these techniques to help many global blue-chip enterprises and organisations plan complex and ultimately successful projects and we have also introduced them to some of the most significant global sports bodies and event organisers but not often enough.

The results have been remarkable. Not only the impact on specific projects but the effect on the individuals who are involved in the process. No matter how much we fight the notion, most of us are, to some extent, prone to doing things in ways we have become accustomed to and comfortable with. But by disrupting established patterns of thought and behaviours and demonstrating that there are new, rational and ultimately more effective ways of doing things you are liberating the individuals involved, enabling and empowering them to think in fresh ways and to be more effective. Doing this visually is up to twenty times faster. It opens up new opportunities and potential from both a corporate and personal perspective and do you know what? They love it.

Structured Visual Thinking™ results in the development of project planning which is based on real-world circumstances and not sloppy thinking. Applied throughout any project and aligned to the use of appropriate technologies in key so-called 'Functional Areas' such as accreditation, media services, security and transport, it ensures that the right type and number of staff are applied to the right elements of a project at the right time and for the right duration. Too often we see staff employed well in advance of them being fully occupied or kept on after their jobs have been done.

In short, it is about creating an intellectual environment in which everything is challenged so that new solutions can be considered, tested and implemented as appropriate. The result is creation of project and management structures with performance measurement and true accountability built-in. That is what event owners and stakeholders will increasingly demand and the sports events industry needs to wake up to that if it is not to be subject to change imposed from the outside.

There's an old description of running major sports events which has been worn almost to death but bares one last airing. It compares running a major event to setting up a Fortune 500 company from scratch, running it for the two months of the event and then closing the whole thing down again.

While there may still be more than a grain of truth in that, the news for the event sector is that those Fortune 500 companies have all changed their acts and (mostly) upped their games by introducing new ways of doing business. Now it's time for sports event managers to do the same.

PLANNING AN EVENT

— LIKE A —

CELEBRITY

JASON ALLAN SCOTT
PREMIER PARTY PLANNER

Over the last two decades I have worked hard to master the art of creating events by blending memory-making moments with business.

So what did I do?

I facilitated the process of turning my client's vision into a reality from concept to execution. Serving domestic and international clients seeking private or corporate event services around the globe, my team and I have designed and produced a variety of events ranging from intimate gatherings for 20 to grand-scale productions for over a million for people like the Pope and films like *Avatar*. As a highly regarded premier party planner specialising in premiers, weddings, corporate and other private work, I pride myself on my ability to perform.

Whether I am designing a private experience for a celebrity gathering or a worldwide cinema release, I strive to create an experience that is memorable, meaningful and engaging for you and your guests and we would be delighted to help with yours in this chapter.

My team and I have grown and keep growing in the hope that one day we can become the premier event consultancy company, servicing clients worldwide. We have tried to set the benchmark in the party planning industry. *We pride ourselves on* providing unparalleled services that are comprised of the most talented, dedicated, creative and passionate individuals with one common goal — ensuring your event is memorable, meaningful and magical.

We treat every client like they are a celebrity whether they are or are not. So without further adieu let us explain how you can, "Plan an event like a celebrity".

Events are a lot like creating a Hollywood blockbuster film. You create the story, the theme, the roles, set the stage and then share its meaning with others. Like most big films, there's usually some organising focal point or narrative that commands the attention of everyone, whether it's a ritual, a meal, or a "starring" guest. But a celebrity event is different.

It is the interactive theatre of entertaining, the sum of energy and motion and people. At an event fit for a celebrity, the action and the stars aren't confined to one moment or one space: the story is open because it is the crowd. But even the craziest kinds of films need directors, and the same is true of a great event. I've been to some with no direction, where people meet, mingle, and network, and leave after forty-five minutes when they run out of business cards. But who can blame them? Yes, a great event can kill lots of birds with one efficient Martini, from mixing different faces and making connections, to kicking off a larger event, or quickly catching up with chums old and new. But if there's no dramatic tension in the room, no sense of movement, what should feel like a party ends up feeling like a product launch or worse yet, an infomercial: you tune out once you see the NutriBullet blend something you thought – un-blendable.

Do not let this happen to you.

You want your party to feel like *the* place to be, and in order to keep it that way, you as the host, will have to give it a plot.

Everyone knows that you can't create a sense of excitement without a little advance buzz, but not everyone knows how to effectively create a well designed invitation that can do this. Mailing out a fabulous invitation that hints at the colour scheme, tone and formality of the party is the equivalent of a glowing advance review. But do not forget: people can't buzz about intangibles. You must also account for all of the nitty-gritty details, which includes mentioning the theme, the RSVP info, the attire, and the full time period of the party, but not obvious things, like the presence of snacks. People want to be in scenes they've already imagined, and if your guests dress the part and plan their time accordingly, they will begin the evening with that crucial spark that plugs them into an anticipated event.

Of course, once they arrive, almost everything else boils down to the creation of a lively space, where people feel fabulous and dynamic both physically and mentally. My favourite way to do this is to choreograph the movement of guests around a careful arrangement of food, drinks, decorations, and each other. And, hey, because we're talking about an event fit for a celebrity, this whole science begins with the bar.

The next challenge will be to keep things fresh. A great event should feel like a volleyball game without the kneepads or grunts – every so often you rotate! Create different situations and stations at your events for different flavours, taking advantage of every surface, and half the dance has already been syncopated. Also, guests who spread out in clusters will not only have more intimate conversations, they'll have an excuse to get out of them when they're ready to hunt down food and flavours. Of course, this clever arrangement doesn't take care of the question of suspense, but I have one other food presentation technique that does: offer your guests a progressive selection of tastes. If you begin by setting out simple morsels like cheese, nuts, and crudités, then introduce a few new items every hour. Your guests will feel a sense of development and, voilà, your narrative is in motion. Another great thing about this technique is that it allows your guests to nibble constantly throughout the event without tiring of the same old thing, an amenity that may be the difference between a bright, wonderful feeling of levity and a terrible feeling of wooziness. On the subject of wooziness, never ever serve potent drinks without food. The elegance they effect so damn well is lost once the room is moving around people instead of the other way around. Once you have mapped out the room through the placement of food and drink, you will be ready to tackle the decorations, another essential ingredient in any great event fit for a celebrity.

Much like food, the idea here is to spread the decorations evenly throughout the venue so people don't perceive any central place to be. Instead of fretting over one centrepiece, scatter decorations and elements of the design motif throughout all active rooms. Do not forget to be practical about the positioning of small tables, where guests can perch drinks and pick up napkins, and the placement of discreet trash receptacles, where they can unload olive pits, cocktail sticks and other refuse. Walking through a room seeing surfaces covered with half-eaten food and wadded up napkins is not sexy, and a celebrity-worthy event should always be a little sexy. The only other fundamental rule of any event like this is dim lighting. On the off chance that your guests have come straight from work, it will either make them feel more glammed up or make them feel less self-conscious. Any way you slice it, low lights create a distinctly loose feel to a space, and will only further encourage motion and mystery.

I must also confess: there is only so much you can do to a space to make it dynamic. After a certain point, you have to create movement the old-fashioned way, with your own two feet. No event is complete without some kind of music, although it should never overwhelm the volume of the conversation in the room. And because music always tends to make people move, it helps a lot with establishing a certain energy level. In fact, a live jazz band or singer only increases those good vibrations, but if you hire one, make sure to let forty-five minutes or so pass before they start: This delay will allow guests to settle in and establish their celebratory momentum.

Finally, and perhaps most importantly, is your own movement as the host. If you do not mingle and enjoy yourself, then how can your guests? I always advise my clients to plan out some basic introductions between people they think might get along.

> "Leo, this is Kate, she is a British actress who likes to be drawn sans clothes, throws away diamonds and does not like to share."

> "Kate, this is Leo an American actor and activist who is scared of bears, will literally die for those he loves and will at some point cry in your presence."

My advice is short quick introductions and then move on, do not get caught up in long conversations (unless you want to!), you simply forge a connection and move about the room. Another great trick for greasing the party wheels is enlisting a partner: everyone has at least one gregarious friend who just radiates warmth; put him or her to use. This strategy will be particularly helpful in the last half hour of the party, when you should finally break all the previous rules and station yourself at the door to say goodbyes, arrange car services, defuse any parking crisis, help with coats and be the last memory of the event.

Just as you should always be the first person your guests see upon arrival, you should also be the last person. After all, at the end of a fantastic film the audience always loves to see who the great director was.

Designing a party that really resonates in someone's imagination is its own reward. Creating an event so wonderful that people with more choice then time choose your event – something that really lives up to the name "event" – is never just about some vision of a party-planning poetry that beams down from the heavens themselves. It is about introducing the tried, the true, and the traditional into your own life to make it new again. I firmly believe that the party itself is only a percentage of the party plan: you should always enjoy every step along the way.

The first step in planning an event is defining your event goals and the reason for the event. Think of your goals as your event's purpose or the reason of its existence. Let's be honest, we may never know the reason for our existence but we must know the reason for the event's. Is it to entertain, to train, to celebrate, to persuade, etc.?

Your objectives are the roadmap to achieving those goals. As I may have mentioned before, the reason should be written out in detail, defining the very detailed, measurable, tangible and later "braggable" results your event will produce. I always say that if you can hire an expert, whether for an event or fixing your basin, then do so.

Any event takes a concerted team effort; the team's work makes your dreams work, handling all of the details. Consider identifying one person in your group as the party planner then subdivide the rest of the group into subcommittees and event managers to handle the venue management, publicity, sponsors, talent, VIPs, entertainment, speakers etc.

For me there are **six ideal ingredients** for the perfect party: **People**, **Music**, **Amenities**, **Food**, **Drink** and lastly the **Lighting**.

Sounds easy?

You need to keep playing around with these elements, like a Rubik's cube, to get them perfectly aligned to create the perfect party. For a great atmosphere you need to pay attention to every detail. You cannot put a price on a good party. However it costs a lot to throw a great party, which is why I often look for sponsors for my events. I once threw a party for a certain celebrity who did not want to pay a penny for his lavish night that included a black-tie dinner and a seven-man band on a boat on the Thames.

When it comes to parties, I like Pinterest, as you can share your vision and concepts so that everyone has a clear idea of what I am looking to create. I find this sharing of ideas through images brings everyone together and creates the excitement around the event.

The key to a premier party is that no matter if you are a celebrity, or a pal of one, you and everyone else feels relaxed and open to having the best time of their lives. I try and go with themes even if it may not be obvious to everyone attending. It is important to every party to have something interesting and unusual the guests can get involved in – it helps get people together and makes the event more then an event but a lasting memory.

I always say we are not in the event-making business but the memory-making business. I have had parties where you would swear I put the "J" in "J Gatsby" with performers from Cirque du Soleil and dancers appearing in the toilets to create drama. Something fun and entertaining ensures that your parties get talked about long after the event is over. I have thrown parties where sports personalities, writers, singers and reality TV stars are mixing with my friends from Africa and Asia who are in normal jobs. I believe it's important to invite a good range of people with varied backgrounds and interests, it leads to good conversations. The best parties go on forever because nobody attending wants them to end. The question of ratio often comes up and my secret is to always have a ratio of two women to every one man.

Women know how to party.

No details should ever be overlooked – and that includes the invitations. I have done scrolls in bottles, video invitations, strippergrams, words branded into sculptures and onto glass and cloth, as well as puzzles. Always look at producing a really great and unusual invitation. I once went to a charity store and bought all the figurines, ripped off the arms and legs and sent them with a note saying, "I would give an arm and a leg to have you attend my gala!".

I always wear a suit or something that is versatile for an event; most times I will have a spare suit at the venue to mix it up or in case someone spills something on me. The dress code should always be noted. I find that "sexy formal" is always the best. When you dress, think about your entrance, the type of image you want to convey and what energy you want to put out as you enter a room. If you feel it, your audience will too. The perfect time to make an entrance as the host/hostess is an hour to an hour-and-a-half into the event. However, if the time is structured then be on time, anything else is just rude. I do, however, believe the best parties are the ones that evolve from their own momentum. They start at 6pm and finish at 5am. Those are the events which test your commitment and staying power and separate the weak from the strong. Know that every detail counts, from the moment they arrive to when they climb into cars and leave – and you are in charge of it all. It is all about making the event a fantasy. At the moment it is all about the green. No, not the money but the bloom. Plants and flowers and the farmhouse look. Instead of 2000 roses why not go with ferns and lanterns and viburnum. Surprise people with raw and rustic when they expect glamour and vice versa.

Tequila is the new vodka and always have a free bar.

Comfort cuisine is always haute. You know you can be bang on trend with cocktails but the main course is still best served traditional – filet mignon, lobster, etc. People love comfort food, there is no getting away from it, so throw in mac and cheese sides or fried chicken as an option. Gluten-free is very big right now but vegan less so. While on trends, the latest one is rooftops because space is so expensive. Venues are popping out from everywhere and Airbnb has as many venues as the old listing platforms and magazines.

Rookie mistake: Long speeches and cocktail hours that go on forever. Both kill the momentum of a great party.

I have a host of DJs that I like to use as a great DJ can save an event. The best music to get a party started? Play any Michael Jackson and people are going to get up and dance – especially Rock with You – and play Biggie (for the young 'uns) and they will dance too. Want people to get close? Marvin Gaye with Here, My Dear and Distant Lover.

Even the best parties can hit a speed bump, and when that happens I take care of things. One of the best things to do is propose a toast – it gives people that pep in their step and revitalises the room. Remind everyone how fortunate they all are. Occasionally I have been known to start a popular phrase or song depending on the crowd which gets "buy in". For example "...The Roof...The Roof is on...." I always send people off with a goodie bag, the best ones will have one personal and memorable item in it. With Facebook and Pinterest it is not hard to see what people like, and who does not love something for free that they have had their eye on? I also always try and organise a taxi service to get everyone home safely. One of the best parties I organised started with a few film people and ended with me and one of the stars, as well as a few lapdancers, on a rooftop where we watched our shadows flickering against the wall in the early hours of the next morning.

The best parties are the ones where you lose your inhibitions or your notions of what you like and who you are and just go with the flow. From my perspective, planning a gathering has all the same charm as attending one: sharing something you value with others. In the end, however, the "celeb worthy party" still depends less on guidelines than on recognising a personal connection between yourself, your guests, and a totally unique occasion. Make sure, too, to stop and take a moment, to look across the venue, look at the faces of the guests and the memories you are creating and have created.

It's in those little moments when you feel that overwhelming happiness radiating from a guest or a group of them, that is when you know you have done it all right.

That is truly how to plan a party like a celebrity.

@Penthouselord

EXPERIENCE

— IS —

BIGGER

THAN JUST THE EVENT

BONNY SHAPIRA
LEADER, CISCO LIVE EMEA

I think to people outside of the events industry, it can often seem a complete mystery as to what we actually do. Because when you attend a good event, it seems pretty straightforward and effortless, and it isn't immediately obvious the sheer amount of effort, energy and hard work of so many people that is actually behind it all.

I'm currently an Event Marketing Manager at Cisco, and for the last two years I've specifically been the lead on planning and delivering Cisco Live EMEA. But I'm an engineer by occupation, and before that I worked in many technical jobs around the different marketing roles at Cisco. It was completely by chance that I got to join the events team. In fact, one of the biggest changes I noticed when stepping into the events role was the equality in the male to female ratio of event professionals. In engineering roles, I found most of the team to be male, yet in events the split seemed to be more or less equal, which was a complete change for me. It definitely added a fresh dynamic to the team and allowed a lot of room for innovation.

I would say this is an incredibly vibrant industry, with lots of peaks and dips and a lot of challenges. But overall I think the most important part of it, and why I love it, is that it touches the real human part of people. We reach, impact and influence a lot of people in what we do, and even if those people don't realise the amount of effort we put into an event, as long as they're happy and leave with a feeling that they've learned something and/or their perspective has been altered in some way, then that's what makes us proud of what we do.

From Cisco's perspective, an 'event' is just one component of the experience. The experience is every single touchpoint that the customer has with the company or with the brand, right down to the small things like whether a phone call comes from the account manager or a call centre. So experience is bigger than just the event, but I would say the event is one of the main touchpoints that will have the biggest impact on the overall experience the customer has with the brand.

The tricky thing with experience is trying to define the success of something incredibly hard to accurately measure. I'd love to meet a person who has developed a clear formula to measure real ROI of an event, because we're just not there yet. In this industry we've not yet developed a way to quantify experience, but what we do at Cisco is to pay a lot of focus on getting as much feedback as we can about the event that we're driving, without making attendees work too hard to provide it. We ask them to fill out a survey after each session that they attend in which we ask them specifically about that session. But then at the end of the show we also ask them to fill out what we call an 'End of Conference Survey', in which we measure a couple of parameters that we can really relate to experience.

These include their general sentiments toward Cisco, towards our leadership, how well they thought the event went, and whether it was a good use of their time and money. We also undertake a pre- and post-event survey, so about a month before the event and two weeks after, we send out surveys to those who have registered or attended, asking them to answer some additional questions and then we compare the results between the two to see if there is any difference. And, usually, we do find that there's an increase in the majority of the parameters – which goes to show that the event was successful.

One of the other parameters that we measure is tracking pipeline acceleration and pipeline creation as a result of attending Cisco Live, so we don't just measure sentiment, we look for opportunities that occur as a direct result of a customer attending Cisco Live, perhaps seeing a new product that wasn't available before and then finally at the end of the day making a booking. So we do track that as well because one of the most important parameters of a successful event is the bottom line: how many dollars did the event generate? So we do the best we can to judge the success of our events. We're not there completely because we know that the impact of Cisco Live is way bigger than the current number we see in bookings.

Another hugely important task when planning an event as huge as Cisco Live is figuring out how to balance the needs of our senior stakeholders with the needs of our audience. With an event that costs each delegate roughly €2000 for the week excluding flights and accommodation, we always begin by putting ourselves in the minds of our typical attendees, and try to evaluate why they are attending and what exactly it is that they expect to get out of it, that they are willing to spend not only their money on, but also one whole week out of their busy year to focus on Cisco.

So, first of all, we try to ensure we give them the things they came for. With that in mind, we still need to look at the needs of the stakeholders, but we do it in a way that is not intrusive. The majority of our attendees are technical network engineers and they come to listen and to have interaction with our engineers and developers face-to-face, which is invaluable for them. We're still able to provide a marketing platform for ourselves, but we make sure it's not in a higher volume than is necessary, so the majority of the time delegates get what they came for, with insertions/shots of what we want them to get. The events team is in place to maintain that fine balance between what our stakeholders want and what our customers want.

In planning, we start to plan the next Cisco Live as soon as the previous one is over for the year. We have a unique and deep relationship with our agency, George P. Johnson (GPJ), and we remain very involved with the planning of the event. We don't treat it as agency side and client side, we see it as one big team working together, and because we outsource a lot of roles to them we spend a lot of time with them. We drive the planning of the event but there are areas that GPJ take full control of, however we're always aware of all of the finer details, which I don't think is necessarily the norm in the industry. We don't outsource everything because it's such a big and important event; we have to be very careful in monitoring every decision that is taken, making sure it is contributing to the overall experience of our delegates, and making sure we keep within budget.

I think there have been discussions for the past few years now about whether physical events will still be around in the future, but we keep seeing the importance of the physical event still growing. Even in these highly-connected times where you can do everything over the internet, there's still no replacement for real, face-to-face interaction. And I think moving into the future it will continue to be the same, and people will always still be drawn to physical events. With Cisco Live, for example, we record most of the sessions and make them available online for anyone to see, two weeks after the event. 95% of the sessions we deliver on site are available online. But still people come. And year-on-year, even as we become more technologically advanced, we continue to see increases in our numbers, and last year we had the greatest number of attendees we've ever had. People come because when you're at an event it's not just sitting and listening to a presentation, it's interacting with people, it's the one-on-one engagement with other customers and peers like you which have the same challenges. It's the experience, engagement and education all together which is combined at an event, which can only ever be done in real life. That's why I'm confident in the future, events will pretty much look the same. The only thing that will change is technology. Tech will change the experience of the event a lot and will enhance it in ways that perhaps we can't imagine now.

One of the main examples we're seeing people increasingly excited about is the advent of virtual reality. I think at the moment it's not much more than a nice gimmick. It's not really a critical part of the event. You see virtual reality demos and interesting displays, but right now, it doesn't really have a critical business role or impact on the event. But, fifty years in the future, could we just be sat at home and put on the glasses and participate remotely in a virtual space without physical location? To some degree perhaps, but, I don't believe we could ever invent something which would replace the value of the real human experience. And as long as we don't all become robots, physical events will continue to exist and prosper.

TECHNOLOGY
MAY FACILITATE
AND

ENHANCE A REAL

HUMAN

EXPERIENCE,
BUT NEVER REPLACE IT

MARK SMITH
MARKETING DIRECTOR, GSMA

For me, events are a combination of a marketplace, a platform for innovation and ideas, together with a touch of show business. I think for the audience an event should be something which stimulates them and brings them together with other like-minded people. But, at the end of the day, it's about bringing people together for a reason, and the reason is for them to do business. An event is something which engages, attracts and compels people to come and be a part of something, but with a view to having a tangible business result at the end of it.

I've been in a variety of roles across the industry but I'm currently Marketing Director at GSMA, a trade association representing 800 mobile networks in 220 countries, which also owns and produces the annual Mobile World Congress for the industry. I work partly in developing new initiatives and innovation around the mobile experience, but I also work very closely with, and actually drive, a number of events within the events side of our business. Our role as an association is to advance the value of mobile communications around the world, and the events business is a key platform for making that happen.

Over the last decade or so, mobile has been a game-changer in almost every industry. From energy to automotive, health to finance, and, for example, how we make payments, the way we use airline tickets, the way we control our cars and monitor our fitness, the way machines interact with each other. A lot of this is still relatively nascent but it's changed the world, there's no doubt. And it will continue to change the world in every aspect.

I began in communications by writing about technology and the impact that it would have in the future. At that time, in the early 90s, the world was analogue and the idea of digital communications – which was just a concept back then – meaning you could actually see a video of someone across the airwaves or that you could send messages without any wires, it was akin to *Star Trek* at that time. It was science fiction and it felt like we were on the cusp of something extraordinary.

But, I knew there was something that was going to be real here, and I knew it was going to make a huge difference to the way the world communicated. And to think in twenty years it became not only real, but a massive leap forward from where we were with telecommunications then; making phone calls from phone boxes. Now 4.7 billion people around the world are using mobile technology and there's only an increasing range of ways it can be used to enhance, change and save lives. We're only at the beginning, starting to scratch the surface of what technology can do.

I think also people often forget that mobile technology is one of the best examples of European collaboration, in terms of developing the digital standard that went global, and enabled this revolution in mobile communications. I've witnessed all of it, and seen it grow from tens of people using it to billions of people using it in every industry in the world. We've been an instrumental part of that, and our event – the Mobile World Congress – is absolutely tied into not just making the most of what our industry has achieved, but advancing the value of it to people, business and communities everywhere. Truthfully, I never could have imagined it would have achieved the scale that it has today so quickly. It took us ten years to reach the first billion people around the globe and then suddenly we hit the next billion in about two years. It's been astonishing.

I certainly believe that technology and in particular mobile will continue to replace many things, like your wallet and your need for credit cards and things like that. But I don't believe technology will ever interfere with the human experience, and certainly will never be the end of events. It's like when people suggested that television was going to kill the cinema industry, it didn't because people do like going and sharing that experience, and that's part of human nature.

In terms of our events, technology is our lifeblood, that's what we do. So from that perspective we have hundreds of thousands of like-minded people in our audience who live and breath technology, and are much more open to embracing it. But that said, we never integrate new technology into the way we put on events unless it's tried and tested. We don't ever utilise something because it's novelty.

In recent years for example, the idea of near-field communications in ticketing has been a major part of what we talk about, and we have moved to mobile-based ticketing and mobile-based user experiences in the way that you access events. But it hadn't really reached the point of maturity until very recently and that's why it's only in the past couple of years that we've implemented it into our events. We don't just implement the latest thing because it's the next big thing. Often we will experiment, but we tend to wait until something reaches a level of maturity, passes critical mass, so that we can guarantee an optimal experience from them.

One of these new technologies which seems to be the buzzword of this year is Virtual Reality. Particularly at Mobile World Congress this year, it was on almost every stand. And I think it's incredibly exciting and the opportunities with it will be mind-blowing, but as for using it to replace events themselves, I'm not at all sure. In the first iterations of web technology, I remember seeing all this buzz around the future looking like virtual exhibition experiences and virtual conferences…but I don't think that humans will ever not have a desire for physical interaction, and to experience something for real. Truthfully, I just cannot see Virtual Reality taking over from event experience in the near future – though I do think Augmented Reality will be a huge enhancement to the event experience. Technology may facilitate and enhance a real human experience, but never replace it.

I've been involved in Mobile World Congress since the very beginning, so for the past twenty-one years now, and we've seen a rapid change in not only the industry but the world, and our increasingly important role within it. Every year when Congress is over I have such a sense of pride in what we've achieved, growing it from when we first arrived in Barcelona which was around 60,000 people, and this year we just hit 101,000. But for us it's not about quantity, and if I look at the quality of the audience this year, we're growing the number of those which are senior leaders and decision-makers to around 57% of our audience, which has grown about 4% or 5% since last year. So we're not about just growing because we need to demonstrate higher numbers every year, we're about growing the quality of our audience too. And when you see the media coverage that comes out of Congress every year, you realise this is something that the world watches to see what happens next.

This year there were so many things to be proud of, whether it was the three times Formula 1 World Champion Lewis Hamilton standing up there, who I would never have believed we could've got engaged in a technology show, or whether it was Mark Zuckerberg returning for his third year. To have someone like that who has a business like Facebook and has been a big pioneer of the way people communicate around the world, was a complete wow factor.

Looking at other pioneering events in this industry, one of the most successful out there right now has to be the TED events. They truly ripped up the rulebook in the way that events are created. There's a certain exclusivity around them, but I think they stripped away so much complexity and really created something extraordinary in terms of the event business model and context for attracting audiences of the calibre they do. When they started livestreaming talks, for free, it didn't have a single negative impact on attendance of their events, in fact quite the opposite. It shows how technology can enhance events, increase value and quality and extend a brand's value enormously. The premise is so beautifully simple and beautifully succinct – ideas that change the world. And it's not only an amazing concept but I think it shows that less is sometimes more in an event. It doesn't have to include everything, but it should be something which is ultimately compelling. And I think they've done that more than any other event I can think of in the last twenty years.

I attended one about five years ago in Edinburgh and that's when I genuinely realised that they are the future. People are really interested in the person and their ideas, and their ability to describe how it can change people's lives or businesses. And that's the crux of it. People are interested in how something came about and how they overcame challenges to achieve it. It's incredibly emotionally appealing and engaging.

When we talk about engagement, I don't think we should differentiate it from experience. They should be one and the same thing. Engaging people is easier the first time you do it. It gets harder to do it the more times you put on an event because you have to innovate, you have to show tangible evolution, you have to enhance and listen to what your audience wants. And I think it gets harder and harder as time goes on if you've got a very successful event because you have to live up to your previous success, and sustaining that whilst making a difference in how you deliver it each time is the critical thing.

But failing, I think, can also be one of the most important things you learn from. Failure can be a lot of things: lack of attendance, lack of engagement, bad feedback at the end; I think at any hugely successful event, something along the line will not work as well as expected, or even fail. One of the things about us which I think is a unique challenge is that we have an incredibly complex and diverse audience. Whether it's representatives from other industries, government ministers or our own association members – we have a massive range and so we must customise and create tailor-made different aspects of our event. We have 300-400 separate, major meetings and sub events that take place over four days – some full-day summits, workshops, seminars and other meetings between key stakeholders on projects – so we customise and tailor-make different things for different audiences within our industry. And it's incredibly labour intensive and it takes a lot of work by a lot of great people. In that environment, any element of that can go wrong. Anything can fail, it's like a fine-tuned watch in that all the parts have to sync together in a precision movement.

But learning from minor failings is one of the most important things for growth. Because that's the easiest way we can work out how to be not only better, but the world's best.

THE

OF
ENGAGEMENT

PETER WARDELL
MAGICIAN, SPEAKER,
AND FOUNDER OF
UNCONVENTIONAL SPEAKERS

Roughly 30 years ago I stood at the edge of the piazza in Covent Garden. I was wearing a purple suit and clutching a battered suitcase. My heart was beating, my palms were sweaty and my head was spinning. I looked out at the people milling around one of the world's most famous street performing pitches and I realised that even though I had a show I didn't have an audience. What was worse, I didn't know how I was going to get one. I had watched other, more experienced performers and they seemed to instantly draw people to them – that, I thought, would be the easy part. I was wrong.

Without an audience I was just a shaggy-haired wannabe in a purple suit.

Succeeding on the street, I learned, was not about my technical skills as a magician. It relied more on my ability to engage with an audience.

What follows are five lessons that have helped me understand how to better engage with my audiences, from the street to the stage, as a performer and as a presenter.

There's magic in them I promise.

THE LESSONS

LESSON 1. MAKE A DIFFERENCE

At the end of my first season of not making any money as a street performer I had this conversation:

"Why do you want to perform on the street?" Dave asked me.

Dave was a veteran street performer. He had one of the biggest shows in Covent Garden and had decided to help me.

"Because I want to make money from performing." I replied.

"That's your problem," said Dave. "You've got your thinking upside down. It shouldn't be about you it should be about the audience. I've watched your show and it's a little desperate, don't you think?"

I didn't know what to say. I felt a little put out by his honesty, but deep down I knew he was right.

"So what should I do?" I asked.

"It's simple," Dave replied. " Focus on making a difference to them not on making money. No one has to stop and watch your show and even if they do they aren't obliged to pay you for it. You have to make a connection with them that is more than just a business transaction. You have to engage them on a personal level. It's the little things that make a big difference.

That's what makes the street such a fantastic place to perform. You have the ability to make a difference to people, live and in person. If you simply show them some tricks they might as well be at home watching TV. This isn't just live entertainment, it is entertainment that's Alive!"

It was all true. I was so focused on doing the tricks that I thought would bring in the money I had relegated my audience into second place. If I was honest I saw them as a "necessary evil" and a bit of an inconvenience. I was polished in the mechanics of my craft but failing in the art. I was neglecting the reason I started performing magic in the first place – to amaze people.

Once I began to shift my focus the show took on an entirely different life. I relaxed and I started to enjoy myself. I was doing less magic but as a result the magic I was doing became more engaging and, well, magical.

What's more, the response I was getting from my audiences was changing. Not just during my performances, but after the show as well. Before, people would drift away, now they were asking to have their photographs taken with me, some even asked for autographs! I started noticing familiar faces in the crowd – people were coming back! Not only that but they were bringing friends with them. I had fans! It was difficult to comprehend. My show structure was essentially the same. It was the same pitch, and the same props. What had changed was my intent. I had learned to see my audience as the engine that powered my performance.

Remember: Your audience are everything, they drive your event as much as you do.

ENTER CELLINI

One of the most influential people in my career as a street performer was Jim Cellini. Known as "King of the Road" Jim was an American magician who had studied under some of magic's most legendary performers. I am lucky to have known him.

The key lesson I learnt from Jim is one that he shared with me as I was voicing my frustrations at not getting the financial results from my shows. I knew I had the skills, the presence and now the motivation to create a great show but something still wasn't happening for me. The problem I was having, Jim explained, was one of scale. I was trying to do the "Big Show", when the secret was to do the elements of the "Big Show" instead. It was structure I was missing and Jim broke it down for me, and introduced one of the most powerful lessons in street performing.

"A street show is about four things," he said, "Make them Stop. Make them Stay. Make them Watch. Make them Pay."

The next four lessons are based on "Make them Stop, Make them Stay, Make them Watch, Make them Pay." They are composites of things I've learnt over 15 years of street performing and although Jim was the inspiration they are not his words. As I was writing this I could hear Jim's voice in my head but I could also hear the voices of so many other performers that I have met, performed and travelled with. Their contribution is equally as valuable and appreciated.

LESSON 2. MAKE THEM STOP – ATTENTION & ATTRACTION

"Every body remains in a state of constant velocity unless acted upon by an external unbalanced force".

If you want to stop some "body", you have to be that unbalanced force. If you think too long about the consequences of stopping a stranger in the street you may convince yourself that it is actually quite a frightening prospect. Fear will start to override your motivation. You need to remain unbalanced. It's the state of falling forward that allows you to start. It is that simple and because it's so simple people dismiss it and look for more complexity where none is actually needed.

Getting people's attention is simple.

If I wanted to stop you in your tracks, I could jump out from behind a tree in a chicken suit. I would get your attention but you would react in an equally severe but opposite direction. You'd run, and I wouldn't blame you.

Cellini explained to me the three key elements to attracting attention: colour, sound and motion. The obvious approach is to increase each of these and become a loud, colourful blur of motion. In live performance the result is a bad clown. They bombard you with noise and colourful props, constantly prodding and poking, dancing around looking for a way through your defence. Contrast that to one of the greatest clowns who ever lived, Charlie Chaplin. He was black and white, never said a word, and could reduce an audience to tears or create uncontrollable laughter with a simple well-timed smile.

You can find examples of the most extreme use of the three elements in most major cities of the world in the form of human statues. Pure white, silent and motionless. They attract enormous crowds, they are the perfect unbalanced force. An empty space that draws you in as you try to fill the void with your own imagination.

So rather than seeking to get attention by pushing out, I had to learn to attract attention by drawing in. To do this I had to avoid directing all my energy towards people, head on. By approaching people at a tangent I learnt that I can soften the impact and still attract attention.

Don't shout "Hey do want to see a show?". That's too direct and you know what the reaction will probably be. Say "Hello" instead, and smile. Do something that breaks away from everyday expectations and that interrupts the patterns of the environment. It can be subtle and although people may not be drawn directly to you, you will knock them into an orbit. That's the beginning of attraction through engagement. Watch any good street performer as they start their show. If you look outside of the performer's immediate area you will see people stop, trying to assess what's about to happen. These people are in orbit and the seasoned performer knows it, looking up and acknowledging these opportunities.

Remember: The secret to getting attention is to pay attention – Look Up!

LESSON 3. MAKE THEM STAY – GENEROSITY & GRATITUDE

Now you've got to build a crowd and turn those orbiting bodies into an audience.

The first thing you need is boundaries. You need to know exactly where your edge is going to be. When you watch street performers laying down their rope or drawing a chalk circle that's what they're doing – setting boundaries.

Your "edge" is the place where your audience will eventually stand but it is far more than a performance area. It shows that you are in charge of your space. It distinguishes you from the crowd. It also makes a promise of something great to come. If your edge is not clearly defined you can quite literally get lost in the crowd. That chalk line controls the flow of energy in and out of your show; it defines you and your performance. It clarifies your identity and focuses your mind, allowing you to think clearly. It places you at the centre of your own universe.

It's important because to generate any kind of interest in what you do, you need people to feel secure. If people feel uncertain they can't focus on anything but the perceived risk. Try reading a book on a high ledge, the ledge will always win in the attention stakes.

They have to know that you know what you're doing. Don't waste time. Give them something!

Jugglers do this all the time. They wheel the big unicycle out onto the pitch at the start of the show and people are hooked. They think "this guy is going to ride that thing and that's something I want to see". So they stay. They don't mind sitting through the smaller tricks now because they know what the payoff is going to be. If someone doesn't want to see the whole unicycle stunt at the end, maybe because they saw another guy do it earlier, they'll walk. That's fine. They leave a space for someone else. You can't please all the people all the time and you shouldn't try.

The promise of what's to come is what makes it interesting and it's a promise that you have to keep.

The beauty of this is that eventually you create a snowball effect. You can stop thinking about getting people's attention; your crowd will do that for you. People attract people. Make certain they know just how grateful you are that they have given up their time – focus on them. Your starting edge will help because now you have created a sense of exclusivity; people can't see what's going on as they walk past. All they can see is a human wall and they will want to know what's happening. You've started to build an exclusive club and no one wants to be left out.

The crowd is on your side now. Focus on them. Give them the attention they deserve. Treat them with respect, let them know just how important they are to your performance.

Remember: Give your audience something to get them involved. Be grateful for the opportunity you have.

LESSON 4. MAKE THEM WATCH – IMAGINATION & INVITATION

To be truly engaged with your audience you need to feed off their energy as well as allowing them to feed off yours. It's a two-way street. The best street performers will always be looking for something that will spark an interaction, something from outside of their boundary, something from the audience. By inviting that "energy source" into the show you're strengthening your bond with the audience and you're keeping the energy levels high. People are more interested in themselves than they are in you, it's human nature. If you can absorb them into your performance, you make them feel as though they are driving the show. Then they won't leave, they can't, because it's their show.

In every street performance there is a make-or-break moment. After all of the hard work that has taken place to build the crowd you need to get them to commit to the show. This is the point when the performer invites the audience to take a step closer. They invite the audience in.

Are you sitting comfortably? Then we can begin.

When you start to learn magic you want to be able to pull a rabbit out of a hat on day one but your teacher won't tell you the secret. He insists that you learn to make a penny disappear first. For weeks you practice the simple move but he won't let you near the top hat or the rabbit. Every lesson you see it up on the shelf and every lesson your desire to learn the secret grows. When eventually you get to hold the props and learn the trick it feels like you've been let into the biggest secret in the world. Would it have felt the same if he'd just grabbed the hat off the shelf and shown you the trick? Of course not. That would have devalued the whole thing and you would have felt disappointed.

There would have been no real experience, just an explanation.

Experience is the essence of real theatre. I've talked about the things that make street performing unique: making them stop and making them stay. Once that's done, once you've built your stage and your crowd, now it's showtime. This is when your crowd become your guests. Now you have the most exciting opportunity that any performer could have; the chance to take them on a journey. Of course, you can take them straight to the Emerald City if you want and get them from A to B as quickly as possible. But if you do you'll miss out on the Enchanted Woods, the Poppy Fields and you'll never meet the Scarecrow, the Cowardly Lion or the Tin Man. Where's the fun in that?

Stories are at the heart of every great show. They take the information you have, the skills you possess and give them emotional resonance.

There's a part of your brain that's as old as man himself, it controls the way we feel and learn. It's driven by emotions, like passion, desire, and fear. It's part of the Limbic system and is truly primal. If you can tap into this, your story will make its way into the consciousness of your crowd. Your performance will have the power to make them laugh or cry. When a magician brings out a small child and begins to pull coins from behind their ears, he isn't hoping to amaze the hundreds of people watching – he knows the trick is too small – but the child who is on stage with him will be amazed. The magician understands the kid's reactions will convey that sense of wonder to the rest of the audience. The audience is transfixed by the emotional journey of the child and it resonates with emotions so deep inside each of us that they can't be ignored.

Watch the guy on the slack rope as he tries to cross between two pillars. He sways and wobbles, sometimes he falls, but the audience keeps watching. Some of them are anxious for his safety, some just want to see him fail, but when he finally makes it across the rope the crowd goes nuts. Picture the juggler who attempts the big trick. They never get it right the first time, they always miss a catch and drop the clubs. In the end they always succeed. It's the classic plot from mythology played out on the cobbles, conflict and resolution, the hero's journey. You know as well as I do (and if you don't I'm sorry to break the spell), that the slack rope walker practices three hours a day and could sprint across the rope if he wanted, and the juggler can handle far more difficult tricks with ease. The audience probably knows this too, but they are willing to suspend their disbelief. They are on an emotional journey and facts don't count for too much. Great theatre takes place in our hearts not our heads.

Stories are powerful tools that help to build trust. Trust is everything if you want to build relationships and engage. The failed attempts by the performer, the juggler and the slack rope walker, make them more human, more fallible. We trust them more because they're just like us and the same goes for the magician and the kid. When a performer interacts with a child, does it well and with care they become instantly more trustworthy. Today we call it *social proof*.

So you need to tell them a story and it should be at the heart of what you do; just remember to keep them moving towards the finale. Don't dodge and weave so much that they get lost and confused. If they lose sight of where they're headed they may choose a different route, you might lose them down a side road. Clarity is essential. Too much information, too much action and you'll overload them. You might become the annoying clown! Have one big trick, one finale and always be driving towards it. Go through the woods and the poppy fields but don't forget that the Emerald City is where your audience really wants to be and where you are taking them.

Remember: Invite your audience into your world and help them commit to your story

LESSON 5. MAKE THEM PAY – COMMUNICATE & CONVERT

I've seen some great shows that made no money because they didn't do this last bit right. Huge crowds can leave without contributing to the hat. On the other hand I've seen weak shows with very little real content create huge returns because they nailed this part. All of your hard work can leave your audience satisfied and you broke if you don't do one thing – tell them what you want. We call it the bottling speech, it's the pitch for money and it really is a piece of theatre all on its own.

The bottling speech is a self-contained story that has a focus different to the rest of your show. Its aim is to convert your audience into paying customers. You can play it a number of different ways: you can be sincere, you can make them laugh, you can use guilt or you can simply tell them what you want. The most effective way is to use elements of all of these approaches. The thing to remember is that you have to be specific, you have to tell them EXACTLY what you expect them to do. Don't leave any ambiguity floating the air, any loophole that they can climb through to avoid giving you what you deserve. If you think everyone should pay you five bucks, tell them "Five bucks!". If you don't want their loose change tell them "No loose change". It might feel tough and maybe you're not comfortable talking about money but you can either talk to the people who are on your side now or talk to the debt collector later. You're not asking for any more than you deserve and if you are you won't get

THE EVENT PROFESSIONAL'S HANDBOOK

it. **Don't be desperate, be definite.** Put the ball in their court and let them know you expect them to act and how.

As well as a great bottling speech you need great "hat lines". These are the lines you throw out as people come forward to tip you. They keep the momentum going by continuing the performance and will make a huge difference to the size of your hat. You are working the people who are still not sure if they're going to pay or who think they can get away without paying. You make the people who are paying feel great by thanking them out loud and contrasting them to those hanging back. Keep hustling until the audience has completely dispersed and give them more than they expected.

Remember: Your audience are the engine but you are the driver of the experience.

IN CONCLUSION

At the beginning I promised you magic.

"Make a difference. Make them stop. Make them stay. Make them watch. Make them pay" – seems like a harsh approach to live events. But it comes from the streets and that's a tough life.

So here's a different perspective:

Make a difference

Attention & attraction

Generosity & gratitude

Imagination & invitation

Communicate & convert

Thank you!

EVENTS ARE LIKE
— A —
CHEMICAL REACTION

BJÖRN WIGFORSS
MARCOM DIRECTOR FOR
EVENTS, MICROSOFT

For me, the events industry is all about helping people with a common interest to get together. And that can be both physically and digitally. But what's it like to actually work in this industry? It's ranked among the hardest jobs you could ever do from a stress perspective, but at the same time, if you're able to manage the stress, then it's one of the most rewarding careers, because you get to experience things you'd never otherwise have the chance to in life.

I often hear people who do not work directly in events say that "it can't be that hard, it's not difficult", but when they actually get into the project team, for instance a Vice President or a General Manager functioning as the host for an event, and they see what happens behind the scenes, they're always impressed by how complex and challenging the job actually is. And it's really rewarding to get that empathy, understanding and respect from people about what you're actually doing.

What I've come to discover over the years is that no detail is too small, but at the same time, if you don't retain the understanding of the bigger picture, then it's not going to work out. You can't just use the constructive part of your brain to build an event, you have to use the creative brain too, and you have to use them proportionally. Work with your heart as much as your head. And this is the hard part to master because if you're responsible for running events and you're only focusing on the execution, then you're not mapping those organisational skills to your creative skills effectively, and you're always going to have an event that feels inconsistent. The key to success is to hyper-focus on the participants. That might sound simple, but it isn't. You might be the only one within your organisation that really fully focuses on this, so what you have to do is to constantly evangelise the paramount importance of designing your event with your target group in mind, and then get others to follow your line of thinking. The best way to get traction is to start with your project team and your agency partners, because together you hold the key to a successful execution.

When I first started in events, being inexperienced and coming from a content marketing background, I was quite insecure, because I didn't really know how to play the game, and I came in trying to run the whole operation, including logistics and everything. Fortunately I had a team of brilliant event project management professionals who held me back. Soon I learned that we had an "us" and "them" thing going on between us and the agencies. We used to say "we have this agency and they're working for us and we're directing them and telling them what to do". Over time we've changed this culture so today it's very different. It's a purely co-creation model, one team.

When I start a project now, we 'refuse all business cards' and we say, "whatever card you have, it's not valid any more, because now we're all working for this project, so we're all working as one team". It doesn't matter what background you have, everybody here is welcome to bring their knowledge, their experience and their creativity to the table. Nobody is deemed less important. That's the spirit of how we work.

Whenever we kick off a new project nowadays I introduce the greater project team with a model that emphasises the focus on exceeding participants' expectations. Recently I wrote an article about this that I'd love to share with you:

THE EVENT PROFESSIONAL'S LIFE: UNDER PRESSURE TO OVER-DELIVER

You've just done an event and people tell you how amazing it was. At the same time, you've got the next one in the works. You're constantly looking for ways to improve and you feel that nobody will remember how great the last one was if the next one you do isn't successful.

Sounds familiar? I bet this is equally true no matter if you're working on the client or agency side of the business. It's that overarching notion of always needing to improve that makes our blood pressure rise.

So how do we manage the stress? Well, the answer isn't that easy, but in this article I'll highlight a few things that can help.

THE KEY TO STRESS RELIEF IS APPROACH AND MINDSET

For the past several event projects, I've kicked them off by introducing a model that puts the participant at the heart of the execution. It's based on Maslow's hierarchy of needs, but I've adapted it for events. It looks like this:

What this does is force us to filter everything we do through the model and it helps us to see how we can meet and exceed the needs of the participants. It also helps us to identify the things that really matter – the levels 3–5 of the pyramid.

As a level one example, nobody will come again to your event because there's food, restrooms, a hotel room and functioning wi-fi. Of course if you fail on any of these you will hear about it so they need to be done well. The beauty of this model, however, is that it forces you to think about what you can do to add value to the participants' experiences. How does catering it fit in with your event's overall creative approach? What about a little surprise in the hotel room as people arrive? Maybe a nice little message on a restroom mirror that makes people smile (and that is contextual for the theme of your event)? These are all simple things that make people feel more appreciated.

Of course there are tons more examples on how to use the tool. We all know the value of networking – it's one of the key drivers for people to attend events in person, but too often it is forgotten when planning the programme and the format of the session: How do we stimulate dialogue and exchange of thoughts? Do we fill the event days with sessions from day to night? Plan for networking!

You might now ask how this tool gives you stress relief? By hyper-focusing on the needs of the participants and by planning your event with them in mind you KNOW that you will be more successful and you KNOW that the experience will be relevant for your participants!

Define your event objectives with the participants in mind. Quite often it is highly useful to either conduct a pre-event survey, or do qualitative interviews with prospective participants to find out what they're after. It's a great tool also when it comes to the ever-important event effectiveness measurements.

When you do pre- and post-event surveys, and you ask the right questions, you are able to measure the impact of the event. How much did people learn? Do they feel more positive about our brand/company after having participated? Did they deepen their relationship with us? Are they more likely to increase their business with us?

PROCESS AND PLANNING

Being systematic is everything but your processes should be defined so that you know what needs to be done and when to do it. This will save you time and therefore reduce stress.

Far too often the process document becomes a burden, so keep it as light as possible but also make it purposeful.

Make sure that you have a clear work back schedule with key milestones when things are due. Agency-side professionals are often very good at this: if you are on the client side of the business it is worthwhile adopting your agency's time lines and complement it with your internal milestones. If it's too detailed for your needs then make an abstract that can be communicated to all relevant stakeholders.

PRE-EMPTING FAILURES

What if something goes wrong? You can plan well, but it is so often the case that you get a lot of stress from the uncertainty that something might not work. What's the solution?

First of all, always do as much as you possible can BEFORE the event. Don't save things that you can fix until later. This will free up time to solve problems that occur.

Second, rehearse. I don't only mean the stage rehearsals. It is also about running through the whole event verbally with the core team well in advance of the event. This way you will clear out any gaps and you will more easily identify what could go wrong – and do something about it before it happens.

MEANINGFUL TECHNOLOGIES

One of the biggest drivers for event effectiveness these days comes via the digital revolution and new ways of communicating. New technology innovations also can be of great value. It is crucially important to plan the digital experiences as much as it is about planning the onsite execution, and both of these should be aligned in content, look and feel. One of the most stressful situations for event pros is the feeling of not quite understanding how to leverage the event on social media. Another one is the adoption of new technologies. For the former, your company most likely have people that are digital experts. Involve them, make them a part of the core team and plan the communication activities together. For the latter, testing is everything. First evaluate if the new technology adds value (use the pyramid as a filter). Then assess how well it will work, "crash test" it. Then rehearse – before the event, early enough to take action if it for some reason still does not work out.

CO-CREATE – ONE TEAM, ONE MISSION

I did mention agency-side and client-side. However, when it comes to an event project we all work for the same team, we all share the same goals and we all are equally passionate about being successful. Ultimately the event lead is accountable for the event. To make people work for the project it is very important to treat all members – internal and external – equally. This makes the whole experience more fun.

As we all know, enjoying what you do is the best weapon against negative stress.

Have fun doing your next event!

Björn

*   *   *

The events' team and its members, at the end of the day, is what makes it or breaks it. Building a team of professionals is hugely important. So how do I spot talent? It's when I see people in the *doing*. When you see people work, you can see how they work. Not necessarily what they do, but their attitude and their ambition towards how they tackle it. It's not so much the skills, it's more about personality, because you can always build competence but you have a hard time changing a person's attitude and personality if it's not the right fit.

I don't necessarily think grades are all that important. Saying that, however, graduating is always a plus because it shows you can complete a task. The difference really is if you've done your summer job selling ice cream, or if you've done your summer job as a promoter, or even if you've taken on a voluntary job running events for a not-for-profit organisation, that's a very, very good sign. You find quality people by looking at what they've done outside of their studies, as it shows they've been curious and opportunistic – very valuable traits to have.

For individuals, when we have new people coming on board, we do a shadowing program and pair them with a more experienced member of staff. When considering hiring a person for my team, I think more about the existing team members I already have than the person I'm hiring, because if the person is a good fit it's going to be way more successful than if the person is just the best one on paper. Then from that, often when you've hired somebody new, the best, freshest ideas come from them once the dust has settled and they've begun to establish themselves. Three to six months in, you start to get some really great ideas coming from these people if you actually permit them, and treat them as equals. Of course, you have to learn to be good at your job, but I believe your voice is still always as loud and as welcome as anyone else's in the team.

What I think makes event professionals unique is that advancing up the corporate hierarchy is not necessarily what makes people happy. Events is a craft, and you need to be a generalist and understand your business to be successful, but at the end of the day, the honed craft is being able to marry the big ideas of the business with a factual detailed execution, and make that beautiful. So then, is it really important to become, say, CMO? Not if you can pay for your milk and bread every day and love what you do. I don't think the main goal is to always climb the corporate ladder. But, if you *are* on a career path and you want to move up or broaden your horizons, stay curious as to what happens around you, and make sure to gain experience outside the events business, otherwise you'll remain an events specialist. Classifying events people as just 'events people' will get us nowhere. We have a lot of transferrable skills to offer the broader marketing mix and progressing should be open to mentorship and advice from a wide range of professional backgrounds.

But now to the events themselves. Often when we think "how do I engage with my audience?" we fall into the trap of thinking about what we do, not for whom we do it. What we should be doing is turning around and saying "What can we do to make them like us more?" rather than say "This is what we do, they should like this". If you don't think about the recipient of the content, you're not going to hit the mark. Engagement is about having empathy, trying to understand the mind of whom you're trying to impress and it's about creating knowledge. Events are experiences that allow people to feel good about us, and success is when you allow people to learn new things and enjoy new experiences, whilst improving the relationship between themselves, and moving the general attitude toward the client into a positive light.

If you say "we have an event" you set something up, and you create a possibility for people to get together. But when you add the creative and you add the drama curve and you add all the things that only event professionals can understand how to do, that's where you actually get the experience from. The event is the format, the experience is the feeling. It's as simple as that. The event is the pieces you purposefully put together, and the experience is the magic that happens inside of it. It's like a chemical reaction; you can bring together all the ingredients, but you still can't entirely know what's going to happen. From one event to another, what forms the experience will be different, so you always have to think "how do you create the perfect formula, when there's not one formula that fits all?"

For example, when we prepare keynotes for the launch of a product, we know we need a 500-person theatre. We need to have a placement structure so that the media get to be first. We need to have our own host... but then we say "what is it that the media actually *needs* when they participate in a launch event?" More than anything they need a fantastic internet connection, and you know how hard it is to get

500 people on the same wi-fi connection and make it fly. So we realised that if we can implement a great network connection, we can offload the wi-fi network by providing a wired connection for those using laptops. What that means is at some events we have 60% or 70% of participants plugging into a fixed broadband which offloaded the wi-fi and made the whole experience so much better. Around big things like that, we also need to think about the entrance experience, how we make sure the people easily find the venue, that we can provide water bottles on each chair so they don't get dehydrated, how we make sure they don't get bored – deciding it can't be longer than, say, 45 minutes – all these small things blend together to create experience.

By trying to think empathically about the participants' needs, we're going to come up with ideas and solutions about even the smallest functional things that make it more pleasant for them. And so trying to get balance between the stakeholder and audience needs is the same thing because a happy audience is a happy stakeholder. Yet we can't assume everybody thinks about the needs of the audience, so somebody has to be their representative. The only people who can really drive that empathy and bring the participants into the picture is the events team, and we ensure people get a better experience when they come there. Nobody else is in the position to do that.

There's one event we did which sticks clearly in my mind as being a really emotive, personal and successful experience. It was Nokia World in October 2013. Just weeks before it had been announced that the whole mobile handset business had been sold to Microsoft. (In fact, I learned this as I woke up in

Abu Dhabi during the final site visit ahead of the event.) So we went into the event as Nokia, knowing that this was most likely the last first party event we would ever deliver under this name. It was a very emotional time for a lot of us. You can imagine the feeling of being acquired and only weeks on you have to deliver a kickass event. But we were able to translate that as a team into an opportunity to emotionally engage with our audience, and implemented that as a pivotal part of the event, and it became very 'goosebumpy' saying goodbye to the old but also saying hello to the future. I thought it was just so beautifully executed by the team that I even get goosebumps when I think about it now.

And so what does the future look like for the events industry? There are three things I think will become the focus: technology, intimacy and analytics.

We're already benefitting from new technologies every passing day, but in the meantime, I think these huge mega events might shift away to become more local. (This change might even happen faster due to the increased security threats we're facing not only in Europe but in the whole world.) The fact that people need and want to be together isn't going anywhere, but technology can change *how* we get together. What if we could be on a virtual reality server where we could shake hands and sit down together? It's happening. The difference between the real world and the virtual world in terms of experience will become smaller and smaller. At the same time, we'll still want to meet with real people, and because technology will develop in all aspects of life, we'll crave that real intimacy. My view is that new innovations and the need to meet in person will continue to complement each other. I actually believe that there is no conflict here.

Finally, I think budget is always an issue because it stems from the fact it is very hard to measure the impact of the event. Being able to prove that our part of the marketing mix is paying back is fundamental in competing with point of sale marketing, digital marketing and social media campaigns. We need to be able to prove that the investment being made is going to pay back with great impact. We have to be able to justify the investment to continue to be an important part of the marketing mix. We are rapidly becoming a more data-driven sector, so moving forward into the future, it will be crucial that we become smarter with analytics.

THE EXPERIENCE IS THE MARKETING

At EITM we unlock potential and provide a pathway to success. In short, we help businesses to grow.

We are a Growth Agency, with a groundbreaking step-by-step process that will transform the direction and focus of your business. Immersive, interactive and inspirational, the Growth Pathway™ designs and delivers a bespoke programme of tasks that will ensure ongoing business growth.

We believe that we have the ability to create growth in any business and any organisation. We believe that the key to this is unlocking the power of collective intelligence, and we do this by enabling people who think differently to think together.

We celebrate people's desire to grow, their passion for improvement and their hunger for more. If individual growth is the starting point, then collective growth is the reward. In harnessing people's ambition and understanding their perspective, we're able to align the entire business around an aspiration for its future.

We encourage people to think freely and define their path to personal growth. It all comes together in our single-minded objective: business growth.

www.theexperienceisthemarketing.uk

@expthemarketing

SOLUTIONS

The UK's leading business content partner

Creating bespoke books, eBooks and apps

For businesses big and small

Harriman House is a content producer specialising in business and finance. We publish our own range of print and digital products and also offer our unique high quality services to corporate clients, working with them to produce a range of bespoke content solutions. Get in touch now to find the right solution for you!

SOLUTIONS.HARRIMAN-HOUSE.COM

Lightning Source UK Ltd.
Milton Keynes UK
UKHW020624230921
391068UK00010B/305